CHARTING THE END TIMES

PROPHECY
STUDY GUIDE

TIM LaHAYE
& THOMAS ICE

HARVEST HOUSE™ PUBLISHERS

EUGENE, OREGON

Edited by Steve Miller

Cover by Terry Dugan Design, Minneapolis, Minnesota

Chart design by Legacyroad Solutions, Colorado Springs, Colorado

Illustrations by Norma Lane

CHARTING THE END TIMES PROPHECY STUDY GUIDE

Copyright © 2002 Pre-Trib Research Center
Published by Harvest House Publishers
Eugene, Oregon 97402

ISBN 0-7369-0988-5

Printed in the United States of America.

03   04   05   06   07   08   09   / VP-MS /   10   9   8   7

CONTENTS

INTRODUCTION

Bible prophecy is one of the more exciting subjects we can study as Christians, for it gives us a glimpse into the future—a future that is filled with eternal hope, peace, and joy. What's more, because God has a perfect track record when it comes to fulfilling prophecy, we can know with absolute certainty that His prophecies about the future really *will* come to pass!

When we wrote the book *Charting the End Times*, our desire was to present a clear, visual picture of what would happen during the end times, and when. Yet Bible prophecy takes on much more clarity and meaning when we take the time to study it in-depth and interact with it. That's why we've created this study guide—it will give you the opportunity to get an even stronger grasp of God's prophetic truth and what it means to you personally.

You'll notice that not every topic in our book *Charting the End Times* is included in this prophecy study guide. However, the 26 lessons in this study guide will still give you a fully comprehensive overview of God's plans for the future. And we have written this study guide so that you can use it alongside the book or as a stand-alone resource.

We trust you'll be blessed as you join us in mining the riches of God's prophetic truth!

Lesson 1

THE IMPORTANCE OF BIBLE PROPHECY

See page 6 in *Charting the End Times*.

One of the truly unique distinctives about Christianity is that God, in His Word, says a lot about the future. In fact, 28 percent of the Bible, at the time it was written, was prophetic in nature. That is slightly more than one-fourth of the Bible! What's especially astounding is that all the prophecies that have been fulfilled so far have been fulfilled with 100 percent accuracy. No other religious text in the world can make the same claim.

God and the Future

In Isaiah 46:9-10, God states a special ability that no god in any other religion has. What does God declare about Himself in that passage?

What does God say about His counsel?

Read Proverbs 21:1. What does this verse tell us about God?

According to those Bible verses, how well does God know the future? And how much control does He have over world events?

In the Old Testament, there are more than 100 prophecies about the coming of the Messiah to the earth. Through these prophecies, we know that Jesus Christ Himself was truly the Messiah, for He fulfilled every one of the prophecies related to His first coming. What's interesting is that in the Bible, there are *five times more* prophecies about Jesus' second coming than His first coming. If we can trust what the Bible says about His first coming, we have even more reason to be confident that the teachings about the second coming really will happen! There's no doubt God wants us to understand His plans for the future—that's why so much of the Bible is devoted to that subject.

Is Bible Prophecy Too Difficult to Understand?

Sadly, many people today are hesitant to study Bible prophecy because they believe it's too difficult to understand. But let's look at what the Bible says about its own teachings:

Psalm 19:7b says, "The testimony of the LORD is sure, making _____ the simple."

Read 2 Timothy 3:16. How much of Scripture is profitable for doctrine, reproof, correction, instruction, and being thoroughly furnished?

Do you think 2 Timothy 3:16 applies to prophecy as well?

About 95 percent of the book of Revelation is Bible prophecy. What does Revelation 1:3 say will happen to the person who reads and hears the words of this book?

I (Tim) have been a student of Bible prophecy for over 50 years, and Thomas has devoted over 30 years of ministry to this topic as well. We can both say from personal experience that we've been tremendously blessed and encouraged by all the time we have spent studying Bible prophecy. Our hope is that you'll be richly blessed as you come to a greater understanding of God's plan for the future as you use this study guide!

Lesson 2

Understanding God's Plan for the Ages

See pages 7–10 in *Charting the End Times*.

As we learned in the previous lesson, God knows "from ancient times things which have not been done" (Isaiah 46:10). He knows the future and has revealed information about that future, which we can find in the Bible. But before we can get a clear idea of what lies ahead, it's important to consider the panoramic sweep of God's plan for the ages, beginning with Creation and the Garden of Eden and going all the way to the eternal city of New Jerusalem—literally, from a garden to a city. It's in the Garden of Eden that we see the very first prophecy about Jesus, and it's the events that took place in the Garden that help us to better understand the unfolding of God's plan for all time. It's here that we see the origin of life, the origin of evil, and the first glimpse of God's plan to redeem fallen mankind.

In the Beginning

In Genesis 1:26-28 we read the account of God's creation of Adam and Eve. God "blessed them, and...said unto them, Be fruitful, and multiply, and replenish the earth, and subdue it" (KJV).

What command did God give to the man in Genesis 2:16-17?

In Genesis 3:1-5, the serpent entices Eve, attempting to get her to break God's command. According to Revelation 20:2, who is the serpent?

Read Genesis 3:6. What choice did Eve (and Adam) make in regard to God's command?

What was the consequence of this choice, according to Romans 5:12?

Sin separates us from God. The relationship that Adam and Eve once enjoyed with God was now severed. But God already had a plan in place to restore that relationship, and we find the first mention of that plan in Genesis 3:15. Write Genesis 3:15 here:

In Genesis 3:15, God is speaking to the serpent, or Satan. We read that the seed of the woman will bruise or crush the head of Satan. The seed of the woman is a reference to the virgin birth of Christ—as Galatians 4:4 says, "When the fullness of the time was come, God sent forth his Son, made of a woman."

The Conflict of the Ages

So, in Genesis 3:15 we find the first prophecy about the coming of the Messiah, the Savior of mankind. As we continue reading through the Bible, God reveals more and more about this coming Savior. And, at the same time, we see Satan's repeated attempts to destroy mankind. This is the conflict of the ages, and the final outcome of that conflict was determined with the death of Christ on the cross, which paid the penalty for our sin, and His resurrection from the grave, which proves Jesus has conquered death.

While the final outcome of this conflict of the ages has already been determined, with Christ as the victor, the conflict still rages. Every person on this earth has a choice to make: repent from their sin and trust Christ as Savior, or reject Christ and remain in their sin.

Read Revelation 20:10. What is the ultimate destiny of the devil?

Next, read verses 11-15. What is the ultimate destiny of those whose names are not found in the book of life?

Read Revelation 21:1-7. What is the ultimate destiny of those who choose to receive Christ as Savior?

While there is much that Bible prophecy can teach us about the future, there's one thing that's far more important than anything else: What choice have you made about where you will spend eternity? There are only two options: heaven, which Christ is preparing right now for Christians, or the lake of fire, which was prepared for the devil and his angels.

If you have already trusted Christ, you have a wonderful future ahead of you filled with more wonders and joy than you can ever imagine. If you haven't made a decision yet, we urge you to believe that Jesus died for your sins according to the Scriptures, that He rose again the third day, and that you can be saved by trusting in His work on the cross as the only payment that can redeem you from your sins.

Because we are finite human beings, there's much we cannot know about the future. But we *can* be certain about whether or not we are going to heaven. And if we make the right choice, then we have absolutely nothing to fear about the future, for we will be in God's hands. There's no better place to be, for He is the one who controls the future.

Lesson 3

Why Christians Should Study Bible Prophecy

See pages 12–14 in *Charting the End Times*.

Over the last few years, the number of Christians who have become interested in Bible prophecy has increased dramatically. This is wonderful, because there are some great benefits to studying prophecy.

When we travel and speak about Bible prophecy, we still meet individuals who tell us they've gone to church for 20 years or more and never heard a single message on Christ's second coming. We've also met pastors who had never taught on Bible prophecy in their churches and, when they made a decision to change that, their churches became more vibrant and spiritually vitalized.

Let's see what we can gain from studying about the last days.

A Better Understanding of Our Personal Future

Read Ephesians 1:18. What did the apostle Paul pray that we would know?

According to 1 Peter 1:3-4, what is waiting for us in heaven?

We who are Christians have a glorious future ahead of us. If we don't study Bible prophecy, we will never know anything about the riches that await us.

A Recognition of the Need to Spread the Gospel

Read Matthew 13:36-43. Who are the good seeds, and who are the weeds?

When will the harvest take place?

In that harvest, what will happen to the weeds?

While it's impossible for anyone to predict exactly when Christ will return, the signs of our times seem to indicate it could be soon. What's more, none of us knows when we will die. It's frightening to think that perhaps we could suddenly die and discover it's too late to receive Christ and become saved from eternal punishment in the lake of fire.

The study of Bible prophecy helps to promote an evangelistic church that has a genuine and passionate concern for the lost. When we know that judgment could come soon, we are more motivated to share the gospel.

An Incentive to Personal Purity

Read 1 John 3:3. What did the apostle John say about those who hold to the promise of the Lord's second coming?

Look up Titus 2:11-13. What does the grace of God teach us? And what are we waiting for?

Are you living in such a way that you would feel ashamed if Jesus were to take you to heaven today? Why or why not?

An Anchor of Confident Hope in a Hopeless Age

Write a very brief description of what the world is like today.

Now write a brief description of what we can look forward to in heaven.

Titus 2:13 says that we are waiting for the "_____ hope" (fill in the blank). What does Paul's choice of words tell you about the future for believers?

The Benefits of Bible Prophecy

Bible prophecy helps us to better understand the future and realize the urgent need to spread the gospel. It motivates us to personal purity and gives us hope in a hopeless age. Every single one of these benefits can have a powerful impact on your life and the life of the church. Considering these impressive results, it's clear that we *should* study prophecy. And as we will discover in this book, it's not only essential but also exciting!

Lesson 4
THE FOUR PIVOTAL EVENTS OF HISTORY

See pages 23–24 in *Charting the End Times*.

Much has happened in human history. Mighty empires have risen and fallen, powerful leaders have won and lost fortunes, and new ideas and inventions have marked key milestones of change for the better. But ultimately, when we consider the most significant events of all, we can count four. No other events in history are equal to these four. Let's learn more about them, and what they mean to us.

Creation

Read Genesis 1:3. How did God bring light into existence? (Note that throughout the rest of Genesis 1, God brought everything else into existence the same way.)

According to Genesis 2:7, how did man come to life?

Is there anyone else who has the same power of creation that God has?

What did God ask man to do in Genesis 1:28?

Think about God's creation all around you. What does His handiwork tell you about Him?

Adam and Eve's sin had a monumental effect, plunging the whole world into sin and corruption. Their disobedience brought about death and decay. About 1500 years after the Fall, mankind was so corrupt that God decided to destroy everything and start anew with Noah's family and the animals on the ark.

The Flood

According to Genesis 6:5-7, what led God to bring about the Flood?

What was the result of the Flood (Genesis 7:23)?

What promise did God make to Noah in Genesis 9:11-15?

Christ's First Coming

Earlier, we discovered that the first prophecy about Jesus Christ appeared in Genesis 3:15. When man sinned, God was not caught by surprise. He already had a plan in place for bringing man back to Himself through His Son Jesus Christ.

What was the purpose of Christ's first coming, according to Mark 10:45?

And what does John 3:16 say about the purpose of Christ's first coming?

In 1 Corinthians 15:3-4, the apostle Paul gave us a brief yet beautiful summary of the gospel. What did he say?

Where would mankind be if Christ had never come? What difference did Christ's first coming make to our world?

Christ's Second Coming

Christ's second coming—or glorious appearing—is the only one of the four pivotal events of history that has not yet taken place, and it's the greatest story of the future to be found anywhere in the world. No other religion offers anything comparable to Christ's second coming.

What can we know about the timing of Christ's return, according to Matthew 25:13?

Read Matthew 25:31-46. In just two or three sentences, explain what will happen when Christ returns.

Who will rule the earth after Christ's return (see Revelation 19:15; 20:6)? What are some ways that this ruler's kingdom will be different than the human kingdoms of the past?

Having answered the questions about creation, the Flood, the first coming, and the glorious appearing, can you see how each of these four events mark the transition from one major age into the next?

Charting What We've Learned

In the chart titled "The Four Pivotal Events of History" on page 22, there are four blank lines. Write the names of the four events in the proper locations on the chart: Creation, The Flood, The First Coming, The Second Coming.

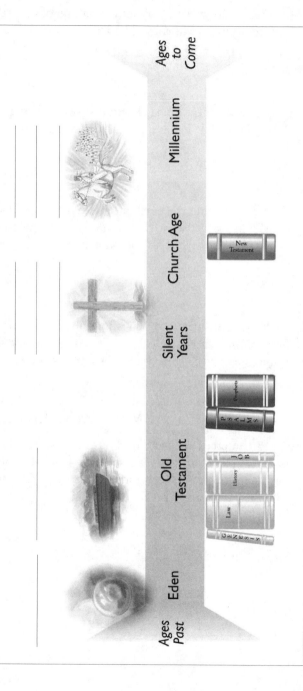

Now look at the horizontal bar that stretches from "Ages Past" to "Ages to Come," and answer the following questions:

What new era was introduced by Christ's first coming?

What new era will be introduced by Christ's second coming?

You'll want to remember these four pivotal events as we continue our study of Bible prophecy, for they help us to better understand God's timeline for both the past and the future.

Lesson 5

THE ABSOLUTE CERTAINTY
OF CHRIST'S RETURN

See pages 24–26 in *Charting the End Times*.

If there is one thing Christians can be absolutely certain about, it is the fact that Jesus Christ will return. The second coming is mentioned 329 times in the Bible, making it the second most frequently mentioned doctrine in the Bible (salvation is first). In John 14:3, Jesus Himself said very clearly, "I will come again." The promise of Christ's glorious appearing cannot be ignored or explained away.

Of the 27 books in the New Testament, 23 have a reference to Christ's second coming. Look up the Scripture passages below, and after each one, write a brief description of what it says about Christ's return, or copy a few key words that refer to His return (keep in mind that the verses below are just a small sampling of what appears in the New Testament!):

Matthew 24:29-31—

Mark 13:24-37—

Luke 21:25-28—

John 14:1-3—

Acts 1:11—

Romans 14:10—

1 Corinthians 3:11-15—

2 Corinthians 5:10—

Ephesians 4:30—

Philippians 3:20-21—

Colossians 3:4—

1 Thessalonians 3:13—

2 Thessalonians 1:7-10—

1 Timothy 6:15-16—

2 Timothy 4:8—

Titus 2:13—

Hebrews 9:28—

James 5:8—

1 Peter 5:4—

2 Peter 3:10—

1 John 2:28—

Jude 14-15—

Revelation 22:12—

The only New Testament books that do not contain teachings on Christ's second coming are Galatians, Philemon, 2 John, and

3 John. The latter three of these books are one-chapter letters, each one written to a particular person, and Galatians does not specifically refer to Christ's return but has an implied reference to the event in 1:4.

Charting What We've Learned

On the chart on page 28, use a pencil (preferably a colored pencil) to shade in the books that refer to Christ's glorious appearing. Don't shade in the four books that don't mention the second coming.

This chart will help you see how much of the New Testament includes prophecies about Christ's second coming. We *can* be certain that He will return!

The Certainty of the Second Coming

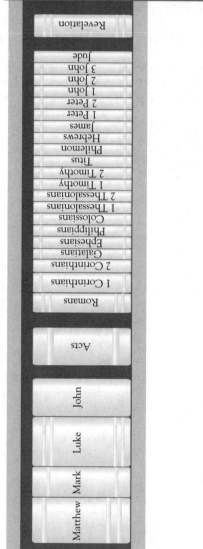

Matthew Mark Luke John Acts Romans 1 Corinthians 2 Corinthians Galatians Ephesians Philippians Colossians 1 Thessalonians 2 Thessalonians 1 Timothy 2 Timothy Titus Philemon Hebrews James 1 Peter 2 Peter 1 John 2 John 3 John Jude Revelation

All but four of the New Testament books contain teachings on the second coming of Jesus Christ. Three of those four are single-chapter letters.

Lesson 6

THE MOUNTAIN PEAKS OF PROPHECY

See pages 26–28 in *Charting the End Times*.

When the Old Testament prophets prophesied about Christ, they did not realize that one prophecy would sometimes contain information about both His first and second comings. When these prophets announced that the coming Messiah would rule the world, their hearers, the Jewish people, did not realize that Messiah would have two different comings. That's why, when Jesus did not free Israel from Roman rule, the Jewish people thought Jesus could not be the Messiah, for Messiah (from their perspective) was supposed to establish a kingdom that would last forever.

We who are alive today, however, have the benefit of looking back in hindsight, and we can see clearly how some Bible prophecies actually have two parts. Some prophecies were fulfilled at Christ's first coming, and others will be fulfilled in conjunction with His second coming.

One Prophecy, Two Fulfillments

Read Isaiah 61:1-3 and write it below.

Now read Luke 4:16-21. After reading these verses, go back and pay close attention to verses 18-19. Did Jesus quote all of Isaiah 61:1-3? Explain.

What did Jesus say next to His listeners in Luke 4:21?

This comparison of Isaiah 61:1-3 and Luke 4:18-19 clearly reveals that only the first part of the prophecy in Isaiah 61:1-3 was fulfilled in Jesus' first coming. The second part has not been fulfilled yet; that will happen when Jesus returns on "the day of vengeance of our God" (Isaiah 61:2b). The day of vengeance, or judgment, has not come yet. That will take place at the second coming.

Charting What We've Learned

Look at the chart on page 31. Above each mountain peak, you will find verses. Look up the verses that appear above each peak. Then look at the list of events below and determine which event should go in the blank line above that particular mountain peak. The six events to choose from are listed below.

Place the events listed below on the correct blank lines on the chart:

Birth of Jesus

Calvary

Antichrist

Sun of Righteousness

The Kingdom

Destruction of the Earth

After you complete this chart, you'll know each of the major themes (or mountain peaks) in all of prophetic history.

The Mountain Peaks of Prophecy

Our Viewpoint
We see the "Mountain Peaks" and the "Valleys" from the side, and we can separate the first- and second-coming prophecies.

Priest
Heb 4:14

The Holy City
Rev 21:2

The New Heavens and New Earth
Isa 65:17; 66:22; Rev 21:1

The Three Appearings

"Hath Appeared"   "Now to Appear"   "Shall Appear"

Glory
Heb 9:24

Dan 7:13-14
Isa 2:1-3
Mic 4:1-2
Hag 2:5-9   2 Pet 3:7-13

Mal 4:1-6

Dan 7:19-27

Isa 53:1-12

Num 24:17;
Isa 7:14; Mic 5:2

What the Prophets Saw

The Old Testament "Valley"—
The viewpoint of the prophets

The Valley of the Church—
The prophets did not see this

The Valley of the "Perfect Age"

Lesson 7

THE OLIVET DISCOURSE

See pages 35–37 in *Charting the End Times*.

In Matthew chapters 24–25 we find one of the most important passages on prophecy given in all the Bible. It's especially significant because Jesus Himself spoke these words, and it's absolutely essential to our understanding of prophecy because this passage provides for us a master outline of the end times. This message from Jesus is known as the Olivet Discourse, and parallel accounts of the sermon appear in Mark 13 and Luke 21.

A Test Prophecy

What's particularly noteworthy is that this message from Jesus begins with a "test prophecy." In Matthew 24:1, the disciples show off the beautiful grandeur of the Temple to Jesus. But what was Jesus' response (see verse 2)?

History records for us that Jesus' prediction in verse 2 was fulfilled to the letter in A.D. 70 when Roman armies took the city of Jerusalem and utterly destroyed the Temple. If Jesus' prediction about the Temple came true, then we can be sure everything else He said about the future in Matthew 24–25 will come true!

The Questions

Jesus was prompted by questions asked by the disciples. The questions appear in Matthew 24:3. What are they? Write them here.

Notice that when Jesus heard the questions, He did not rebuke the disciples for wanting to know about the future. In fact, He encouraged them through His detailed answer. This tells us that in God's eyes, the understanding of prophecy is definitely a worthwhile pursuit!

Jesus' Answer

At the same time that Jesus answered His disciples, He gave an important warning. What is that warning (verses 4-5,11)?

What will believers hear about, according to verse 6a?

How should believers react to this news (verse 6b)?

According to verse 7, what are four specific things that will happen?

What does verse 8 tell us about these four things?

Verses 9-14 describe the first half of the Tribulation period. In brief sentences, write what will happen during this time.

The event described in verse 15 will take place at the halfway point of the Tribulation. What will people see?

What does Jesus warn everyone to do in response to the event described in verse 15 (read verses 16-20)?

How does Jesus describe this time, according to verse 21?

Jesus gives another warning in verses 23-26. What does He caution against?

According to verses 27 and 29-31, what can we expect to happen at the time of Christ's return?

Being Ready

What important announcement did Jesus make about His second coming in verse 36?

As a result, what should we do (verse 44)?

What will happen to those who do not heed Jesus' exhortation in verse 44 (read verses 48-51)?

Charting What We've Learned

Look at the chart on page 36. Read each of the verse references, and using the blank lines, write what will happen at that point of time on the chart. Feel free to use the answers you've already written in this lesson.

Will all the things Jesus describes in Matthew 24–25 really take place? In Matthew 24:35, near the midpoint of His message, Jesus said, "Heaven and earth will pass away, but My words will not pass away." In other words, everything Jesus taught will happen exactly the way He said it will. There is nothing that can change the course of the future. That is yet another affirmation that we can fully trust Bible prophecy!

The Olivet Discourse (Matthew 24–25)

Church Age

Tribulation 7 Years

Millennium 1000 Years

Second Half (3-1/2 yrs.)

The Great Tribulation 24:21-25

Rapture

24:7-8

24:32-36

24:26-31

24:1-3

24:9-14

24:15-20

25:31-46

Timelines of disproportionate length are broken to indicate they are not the same amount of time as other bars in the chart

Lesson 8

PAUL AND THE SECOND COMING

See pages 38–40 in *Charting the End Times*.

There are many different views of what will happen in the end times. The main reason for this is that it's necessary to piece together many different Scripture passages in order to create a chronological picture of what will happen in the last days.

There are some people who believe Christians will not be raptured from the earth until the *end* of the Tribulation, some who teach the rapture will take place *during* the Tribulation, and still others (ourselves included) who believe the rapture will happen *before* the Tribulation.

Is it possible to know for sure what the Bible teaches? While there are some specifics about the end times that aren't very clear in Scripture, we believe that with careful study, we *can* determine with reasonable confidence the timing of the Rapture, the Tribulation, and the second coming.

With that in mind, we're going to spend the next few lessons putting the pieces of the puzzle together and creating a clear picture of what will happen and when. Let's start with 2 Thessalonians 2:1-12, which is one of the few places in Scripture that includes all the key elements of Christ's return in just one passage.

2 Thessalonians 2:1

What two things does the apostle Paul talk about in
2 Thessalonians 2:1?

Pay special attention to the last few words in the verse, "our
gathering together unto him." Let's assume this "gathering
together" happens at the end of the Tribulation. We know with
absolute certainty that at the end of the Tribulation, judgment
will take place (read Revelation 19:11-21).

If this "gathering together" has to do with being gathered
together for judgment, then why is it mentioned *before* the appearance of the Antichrist, who is mentioned in verses 4-8? That
doesn't make sense, especially considering the fact that Christ's
judgment is mentioned later in verse 8 ("whom the Lord…will
bring to an end by the appearance of His coming").

Thus, the "gathering together" takes place *before* the Antichrist shows up. This indicates the Rapture takes place before
the Tribulation.

2 Thessalonians 2:3

What two names are given for the Antichrist in verse 3?

What must happen before the "man of sin [is] revealed"
(verse 3 KJV)?

Let's take a closer look at verse 3. Bible scholars have debated
the exact meaning of the term "falling away" (KJV), which is how
the term is translated in the King James Version of the Bible. The
Greek word *apostesia* can refer to a physical departure. But what

kind of departure is it? Interestingly, before the King James Version was written, there were seven different English translations of the Bible that agreed with the translation "departing first," and not "falling away." These seven English translations were written between 1384 and 1608. In other words, the idea of a departure could actually refer to the Rapture. Not until the King James was published in 1611 was the original Greek text translated "falling away."

Thus, it's highly likely that in verse 3, Paul is saying that the *departure* or disappearance (the Rapture) will take place *before* the Antichrist comes. Some say Paul is referring to people who fall away into apostasy, but that's not how the earlier translators of the English Bible took the passage.

2 Thessalonians 2:4-8

According to verse 4, what will the Antichrist do?

What does verse 8 say the Lord Jesus Christ will do?

And *when* will Christ do this?

Looking at 2 Thessalonians 2:1-12 as a whole, we see the Rapture in verse 1, the man of sin (or the Antichrist) revealed in verse 3, and Christ's second coming and destruction of the Antichrist in verse 8.

So that you can better understand the "timeline" given in 2 Thessalonians 2:1-12, you'll want to study the chart on page 40.

An Unexpected Surprise

Here's another important thought: If the Rapture were to happen after the Tribulation, then anyone would be able to

Paul and the Second Coming

Pretribulation Rapture in One Chapter—2 Thessalonians 2:1-12

The Father's House

Timelines of disproportionate length are broken to indicate they are not the same amount of time as other bars in the chart

Future Ages

Millennium

The Day of the Lord (verses 2, 8)

2 Thessalonians 2:8-10

7-Year Tribulation

Great Tribulation

3 1/2 yrs.

The Rapture "Our gathering together unto Him" (verse 1)

Man of Sin Revealed (verse 3)

Man of Sin Desecrates the Temple (verse 4; Daniel 9:27)

Christ Destroys Man of Sin (verse 8)

Church Age

Past Ages

calculate the exact time of His glorious appearing and judgment of the Antichrist. But the Bible tells us "be ye also ready: for in such an hour as ye think not the Son of man cometh" (Matthew 24:44 KJV). The only way the Rapture can truly come as an unexpected surprise is if it's before the Tribulation, not after it!

Lesson 9

THE RAPTURE OF THE CHURCH

See pages 50–52 in *Charting the End Times*.

The apostles of the first-century church lived with the expectation that Christ could come at any moment. Their writings indicate that the Lord's return would be sudden and unexpected—that's why they warned that all Christians should be ready, "looking for the blessed hope" (Titus 2:13). In fact, Jesus Himself said, "Take ye heed, watch and pray: for ye know not when the time is" (KJV). As we learned earlier, if the Rapture were to take place *after* the Tribulation, then it would not be an unexpected event.

The fact that Christ could come to call us to Himself at any time (see John 14:3; 1 Thessalonians 4:17) is a concept known as *imminency*. In other words, it's an event that could happen at any moment. When we look at all the rapture passages in the Bible, we notice that there are no prophecies left to be fulfilled before the Rapture.

Where Does the Word *Rapture* Come From?

The word *Rapture* originates from 1 Thessalonians 4:16-17, which describes the event in this way:

> The Lord himself will descend from heaven with a shout, with the voice of the archangel and with the trumpet of God, and the dead in Christ will rise first. Then we who are alive and remain will be *caught up* together with them in the clouds to meet the Lord in the air, and so we shall always be with the Lord (emphasis added).

The words "caught up" are a translation of the Greek word *harpazo*, which means "snatched up." The word *Rapture* is not in or from the original Greek text; rather, it comes from a Latin translation of the Bible that was written in the fourth century A.D. It refers to believers being taken up suddenly, without warning, to heaven to be with the Lord Jesus Christ.

Read 1 Corinthians 15:52, which also speaks of the Rapture. What words are used in this verse to indicate how quickly the Rapture will take place?

The Specifics of the Rapture

One reason we can be certain that the Rapture and the glorious appearing are two separate events is that the Scripture passages that describe the Rapture are significantly different from the passages that describe Christ's return at the end of the Tribulation. The two events simply cannot be reconciled. We'll study that more in the upcoming lessons; for now, let's take a look at the *events* of the Rapture.

Look up the following Scripture verses, and after each verse, write a brief note that explains what's taking place in that verse.

1. John 14:3; 1 Thessalonians 4:16—

2. 1 Thessalonians 4:14-15—

3. 1 Corinthians 15:52—

4. 1 Thessalonians 4:16-17—

5. 1 Corinthians 15:51,53—

6. Romans 14:10; 2 Corinthians 5:10—

Charting What We've Learned

By writing your observations, you've helped to make yourself more familiar with some of the key rapture passages in the Bible. Now that you're finished, turn to the chart on pages 46-47. This chart carefully details all that will take place during the Rapture, and mentions the same verses you just studied.

After reading all 15 events listed on the chart, answer the following questions:

What excites you most about the Rapture?

In light of the fact that the Rapture could happen at any time, are there any changes you want to make in your priorities or in the ways you use your time? Write your thoughts below, and offer them up to God in prayer.

EVENTS OF

1. The Lord Himself will descend from His Father's house, where He is preparing a place for us (John 14:1-3; 1 Thessalonians 4:16).

2. He will come again to receive us to Himself (John 14:1-3).

3. He will resurrect those who have fallen asleep in Him (deceased believers whom we will not precede—1 Thessalonians 4:14-15).

4. The Lord will shout as He descends ("loud command," 1 Thessalonians 4:16 NIV). All this takes place in the "twinkling of an eye" (1 Corinthians 15:52).

5. We will hear the voice of the archangel (perhaps to lead Israel during the seven years of the Tribulation as he did in the Old Testament—1 Thessalonians 4:16).

6. We will also hear the trumpet call of God (1 Thessalonians 4:16), the last trumpet for the church. (Don't confuse this with the seventh trumpet of judgment upon the world during the Tribulation in Revelation 11:15.)

7. The dead in Christ will rise first (the corruptible ashes of their dead bodies are made incorruptible and joined together with their spirits, which Jesus brings with Him—1 Thessalonians 4:16-17).

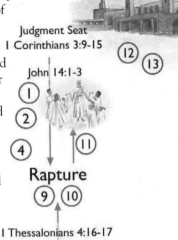

The Father's

Judgment Seat
1 Corinthians 3:9-15

John 14:1-3

Rapture

1 Thessalonians 4:16-17
1 Corinthians 15:51-58

Church Age

Tribulation

THE RAPTURE

8. Then we who are alive and remain will be changed (or made incorruptible by having our bodies made "immortal"—1 Corinthians 15:51,53).

9. We will be caught up (raptured) together (1 Thessalonians 4:17).

10. We will be caught up in the clouds (where dead and living believers will have a monumental reunion—1 Thessalonians 4:17).

House

11. We will meet the Lord in the air (1 Thessalonians 4:17).

12. Christ will receive us to Himself and take us to the Father's house "that where I am, there you may be also" (John 14:3).

Marriage of the Lamb

13. "And so we shall always be with the Lord" (1 Thessalonians 4:17).

14. At the call of Christ for believers, He will judge all things. Christians will stand before the judgment seat of Christ (Romans 14:10; 2 Corinthians 5:10), described in detail in 1 Corinthians 3:11-15. This judgment prepares Christians for...

15. The marriage of the Lamb. Before Christ returns to earth in power and great glory, He will meet His bride, the church, and the marriage supper will take place. In the meantime, after the church is raptured, the world will suffer the unprecedented outpouring of God's wrath, which our Lord called "the great tribulation" (Matthew 24:21).

7 Years

Millennium 1000 Years

Lesson 10

THE JUDGMENT AND REWARDS
OF BELIEVERS

See pages 53–55 in *Charting the End Times*.

Immediately after the Rapture, Christians will find themselves in heaven with the Lord Jesus Christ. It's the Rapture that
will fulfill Jesus' wonderful promise in John 14:2-3:

> In my Father's house are many dwelling places; if it
> were not so, I would have told you; for I go to prepare
> a place for you. If I go and prepare a place for you, I
> will come again and receive you to myself, that where
> I am, there you may be also.

It's important to recognize that the one single purpose of the
Rapture is to take Christians from earth to heaven. In the Rapture, we will meet Christ in the clouds and be taken to His
Father's house. By contrast, in the glorious appearing, Jesus Christ
will descend to earth, pour out judgment on His foes, and set up
His kingdom. Clearly, then, there are two different phases to His
return to earth. In the first phase, the Lord comes to get His
church, and in the second phase, He returns to earth to establish

His reign. We will study more about the differences between these two phases later in the study guide.

The Judgment Seat of Christ

Immediately after we who are Christians arrive in heaven, we will stand before the Lord Jesus Christ to be judged by Him. This is not a judgment related to our salvation, for Christ's death on the cross and our belief in His work on our behalf has secured us a place in eternity. Rather, this judgment is for the purpose of rewarding us according to our works on earth.

In 1 Corinthians 3:9, the apostle Paul says that "we are God's fellow workers." He then goes on to say this:

> According to the grace of God which was given to me, like a wise master builder I laid a foundation, and another is building on it. But each man must be careful how he builds on it. For no man can lay a foundation other than the one which is laid, which is Jesus Christ. Now if any man builds on the foundation with gold, silver, precious stones, wood, hay, straw, each man's work will become evident; for the day will show it because it is to be revealed with fire, and the fire itself will test the quality of each man's work. If any man's work which he has built on it remains, he will receive a reward. If any man's work is burned up, he will suffer loss; but he himself will be saved, yet so as through fire (verses 10-15).

Based on this passage, who is the foundation?

With what materials can you build upon that foundation?

What is the purpose of the fire?

If a person's work endures, what will happen?

If a person's work doesn't endure, what will happen?

Works of Gold, Silver, and Precious Stones

The works that will receive rewards are called "good works." In 1 Corinthians 9:12, Paul described these works as "gold, silver, precious stones"—these will not burn up in the fire of judgment. Look up the following Bible passages, and write what you learn about good works:

Matthew 5:16—

Philippians 2:13-15—

Matthew 10:42—

Romans 12:9-19—

Our Eternal Rewards

Among the rewards we will receive are crowns. There are five different kinds of crowns described in Scripture. Look at the chart on pages 52-53. Below each crown is a Scripture verse. Read each verse and answer the question that follows it.

Imagine your works being tested by fire. What do you think the results would be?

In light of the previous question, can you think of two or three changes you would like to make in your life?

What is one good work you can do *today* for someone else?

The Judgment Seat of Christ (The Bema)
Romans 14:10

Heaven

Christ Meets the Church
1 Ths 4:16-17

The Marriage of the Lamb
Rev 19:7-9

Judgment of Believers for Their Works
1 Cor 3:11-15; 2 Cor 5:10

Gold, Silver, and Precious Stones

Wood, Hay, and Stubble

The Rapture
1 Ths 4:13-18

The Glorious Appearing
2 Ths 1:7-10

Incorruptible Crown	Crown of Life	Crown of Glory	Crown of Righteousness	Crown of Rejoicing
1 Cor 9:25	Rev 2:10	1 Pet 5:2-4	2 Tim 4:8	1 Ths 2:19-20
Who will receive this crown?	Who will receive this crown?	Who will receive this crown?	Who will receive this crown?	Who will receive this crown?

Lesson 11

UNDERSTANDING THE TRIBULATION

See pages 56–62 in *Charting the End Times*.

If you could bring together all the absolute worst times of anguish the world has ever known and unleash them all at once, you wouldn't come even close to the still-future time of intense suffering known as the Tribulation. The Spanish Inquisition, the World Wars, and the Holocaust—all of which were very horrible and tragic—pale in comparison to what's still to come. One reason is that all those events were outpourings of the wrath of *man*. But in the Tribulation, we will witness the outpouring of the wrath of *God*.

The prophet Isaiah referred to the Tribulation as "the day of vengeance of our God" (61:2). Jeremiah called it "the time of Jacob's trouble," a reference to the fact that the Tribulation will bring with it a time of national suffering for Israel. Jesus Himself, when He talked about the last days prior to His second coming, said there would be "great tribulation, such as has not occurred since the beginning of the world until now, nor ever will" (Matthew 24:21). There has never been and never will be another calamity like the Tribulation.

That the Tribulation is a significant event is clear from the amount of space it receives in Scripture. More is said about this period of wrath than about the 1000-year Millennial kingdom, heaven, or hell. The Old Testament prophets mention it at least 49 times, and it's mentioned at least 15 times in the New Testament.

How Long Is the Tribulation?

In Daniel 9:24-27, a passage popularly known as the prophecy of the 70 weeks or 490 years, we discover that the Tribulation period will last "one week," and the Hebrew terminology here refers to a week of years, or seven years. The first 69 weeks of years, which started with King Artaxerxes' decree to rebuild Jerusalem, ended with the rejection of Jesus (a period of exactly 483 years). The last week, or 70th week, is seven years long, which brings us to the full 490 years prophesied by Daniel. However, that 70th week has not taken place yet. We're now in a gap of time known as the church age, and Daniel's prophecy had to do with the nation of Israel.

That the 70th week is still future is clear in Daniel 9:27, which says, "He [the prince mentioned in verse 26] will make a firm covenant with the many for one week; but in the middle of the week He will put a stop to sacrifice and grain offering; and on the wing of abominations will come one who makes desolate." This description is parallel to what 2 Thessalonians 2 and Revelation says about the future Antichrist, who will make a covenant with Israel for seven years (the unfulfilled seven years of Daniel 9), and he will break that covenant in the middle of that week, or the middle of the Tribulation, and desecrate the Temple (which is the abomination of desolation).

Before continuing with this lesson, you'll want to study Daniel's 70-week prophecy on the chart on page 55. Note carefully the location of the first 69 weeks, the church age, and the last week.

The New Testament also tells us about the length of the Tribulation. There, we find the seven years divided into two periods of 1260 days, or 42 months, or three-and-one-half years, or "time and times and half a time" (Revelation 11:2-3; 12:6,7,14; 13:5).

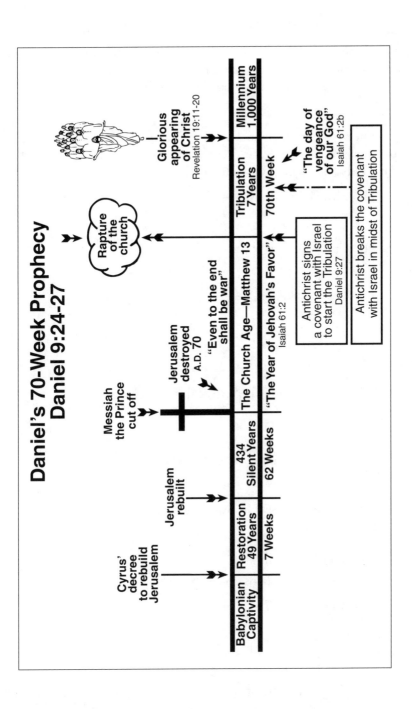

The Judgments of the Tribulation

In the book of Revelation, we find there are three sets of judgments that God will pour out on mankind: the seal judgments, the trumpet judgments, and the bowl judgments.

The Seal Judgments

The first four judgments involve the four horsemen described in Revelation 6:2-8. Read these verses, and describe what effect each horseman will have on the earth:

The white horse (6:1-2)—

The red horse (6:3-4)—

The black horse (6:5-6)—

The pale horse (6:7-8)—

What happens after the fifth seal is broken open in Revelation 6:9-11?

What about the sixth seal in 6:12-17?

And the seventh seal in Revelation 8:1-2?

The Trumpet Judgments

Describe what happens on earth after each trumpet sounds:

First trumpet (8:6-7)—

Second trumpet (8:8-9)—

Third trumpet (8:10-11)—

Fourth trumpet (8:12)—

Fifth trumpet (9:1-11)—

Sixth trumpet (9:12-19)—

Seventh trumpet (11:15-19)—

Bowl Judgments

Last are the bowl judgments. Describe each judgment, and note also the reactions of those who suffer from the judgments.

First bowl (Revelation 16:2)—

Second bowl (16:3)—

Third bowl (16:4)—

Fourth bowl (16:8-9)—

Fifth bowl (16:10-11)—

Sixth bowl (16:12-16)—

Seventh bowl (16:17-21)—

Examining What We've Learned

Based on what you've read about the judgments of the Tribulation, would you say the Tribulation has already taken place, or would you say it's still in the future? Why?

Lesson 12

CHARTING THE TRIBULATION

See pages 56–62 in *Charting the End Times*.

The book of Revelation says a lot about the Tribulation—so much so that at first, it may seem overwhelming to us. But if we study Revelation section by section, we can get a clearer understanding of what will happen and when.

In the previous lesson, we studied the seal, trumpet, and bowl judgments. We're going to place those judgments on a chart so we can get a better idea of how they fit in the "big picture" of the whole book of Revelation. But before we begin working on our chart, it's important for us to answer three questions:

What will the Antichrist do to *start* the Tribulation, according to Daniel 9:27a?

What event will mark the *midpoint* of the Tribulation (read Daniel 9:27b and Matthew 24:15)?

What event will mark the *end* of the Tribulation, according to Revelation 19:11-21?

On pages 62-63 is a chart depicting the Tribulation. You'll notice that the vertical lines for the seal judgments, the trumpet judgments, and the bowl judgments are blank. Using the answers that you wrote in the previous lesson on pages 56–58, write the name of each judgment on the blank vertical lines.

After you have filled in the blanks, you'll want to add three new items to the chart:

- Write "The Antichrist's Covenant" at the beginning of the Tribulation timeline.

- Write "The Abomination of Desolation" at the midpoint of the Tribulation timeline.

- Write "The Return of Christ and Destruction of Antichrist" at the end of the Tribulation timeline.

Understanding the Purpose of the Tribulation

Over the last two lessons, we've taken a close look at the horrible judgments that will take place on the earth during the Tribulation. A question that naturally comes to mind is, Why will God bring all this about? Is it really necessary?

Everything God does has a purpose, and that's true about the Tribulation. While there are actually several purposes, we would like to focus on just one: God will use the Tribulation to force man to choose between Him or Antichrist.

The events of the Tribulation are intended to give all people a very clear opportunity to either follow God or follow Antichrist. For thousands of years, God has given people the choice of worshiping Him voluntarily or rejecting Him. And there is coming a day when God will take the world back as His own and set up His everlasting rule upon it. But before doing so, He will give everyone around the globe an opportunity to accept or reject Him. The Tribulation will make it clear that there's no middle ground—no one can sit on the fence when it comes to their status with God.

God's Mercy in the Tribulation

While the Tribulation is primarily a time of judgment, God will go all out in His efforts to draw people to Himself. Let's take a closer look at how He will do this.

According to Joel 2:28-29, what will God pour out in the last days?

In Revelation 7:4-8, how many Jewish witnesses does God assign to proclaim the gospel?

How long will God's two special witnesses testify in Jerusalem with supernatural power (see Revelation 11:3)?

What does Revelation 14:6-7 say that God will do to reach people?

And how widespread will this effort be?

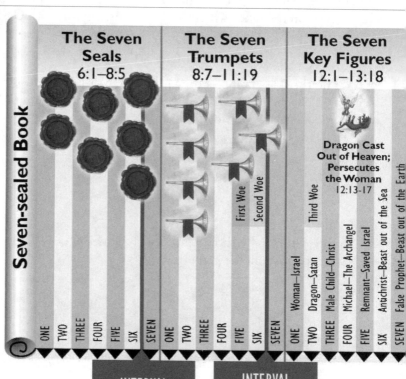

The Seven Seals
6:1–8:5

The Seven Trumpets
8:7–11:19

The Seven Key Figures
12:1–13:18

Seven-sealed Book

First Woe

Second Woe

Third Woe

Dragon Cast
Out of Heaven;
Persecutes
the Woman
12:13-17

ONE — Woman—Israel

TWO — Dragon—Satan

THREE — Male Child—Christ

FOUR — Michael—The Archangel

FIVE — Remnant—Saved Israel

SIX — Antichrist—Beast out of the Sea

SEVEN — False Prophet—Beast out of the Earth

ONE · TWO · THREE · FOUR · FIVE · SIX · SEVEN

ONE · TWO · THREE · FOUR · FIVE · SIX · SEVEN

INTERVAL
144,000 Sealed
(7:1-8)

INTERVAL
Little Book,
Two Witnesses
(10:1—11:13)

Tribulation (Daniel's

First Half of Tribulation (3 1/2 Years)

The Tribulation

The
Harlot
17:1-18

The Seven Bowls 15:1–16:21	Seven Dooms on Babylon 17:1–18:24	Return of Christ 19:1–21	

The Seven Bowls — ONE, TWO, THREE, FOUR, FIVE, SIX, SEVEN

Seven Dooms on Babylon
- ONE — Devoid of Human Life
- TWO — Burned with Fire
- THREE — Destroyed in One Hour
- FOUR — People Afraid to Enter Her Borders
- FIVE — Riches Brought to Nothing
- SIX — Violently Overthrown
- SEVEN — All Activity Ceases

Return of Christ
- Battle of Armageddon
- Marriage of the Lamb
- Return of Christ with the Church and His Angels
- Antichrist and False Prophet Cast into the Lake of Fire

The Millennial Kingdom

INTERVAL
Three Angel Messengers
(14:1-20)

Seventieth Week)

Second Half of Tribulation (3 1/2 Years)

The
**False
Prophet**
13:11-17

The
Beast
13:1-6

These efforts on God's part will bring about the largest soul harvest ever in human history. According to Revelation 7:9, this harvest will yield "a great multitude which no one [can] number."

God's desire is for people to become saved, and He is "not wishing for any to perish, but for all to come to repentance" (2 Peter 3:9). Do you share God's passion for the lost? Are there people you could be praying for right now who are not saved—perhaps family members, friends, or coworkers? Write their names here, and start praying for them today! Ask God for opportunities to "let your light shine before men in such a way that they may see your good works, and glorify your Father who is in heaven" (Matthew 5:16).

Lesson 13

THE CAMPAIGN OF ARMAGEDDON AND CHRIST'S RETURN

See pages 63–64 in *Charting the End Times*.

The final war in all human history—a war that will not take place as planned by its military leaders—will take place at the second coming of Jesus Christ. If you've been a Christian for any length of time, you may have heard reference to the Battle of Armageddon. In fact, even among non-Christians, the name *Armageddon* is often used to refer to some sort of great, final, cataclysmic event.

The Significance of Armageddon

The word *Armageddon* has Hebrew roots, with the word *Har* meaning "mountain" or "hill," and *Magedon* being a reference to the ruins of an ancient city that overlooks the Valley of Esdraelon in northern Israel.

In the Battle of Armageddon, the leaders of the world, headed by Antichrist, will gather their armies to fight against Israel. Through the ages, Satan has wanted to destroy Israel because he has wanted to prevent God's promises from being fulfilled through His chosen people. But Satan has not succeeded, and in the Battle of Armageddon, he will make one last attempt—which will be thwarted by none other than the Lord Jesus Christ.

Let's look at the Scriptures, and see what will take place in connection with the campaign at Armageddon.

The Unfolding of Armageddon

Read Revelation 16:12-16. What happens to the "great river Euphrates" when the sixth angel pours out his bowl? Why does this happen?

In verse 14, what do the spirits of demons do with the kings of the earth?

Where do these kings and people gather (see verse 16)?

What disaster is proclaimed by an angel in Revelation 18:2?

How quickly will this destruction take place, and how wide-spread will it be (see Revelation 18:10,17,19)?

What will take place in Jerusalem, according to Zechariah 14:2?

What will God cause to happen at Bozrah (see Micah 2:12)?

Read Zechariah 12:10 and Romans 11:26-27. What miraculous change will take place among the people of Israel?

Read Isaiah 34:1-8. What clues in these verses reveal that we are looking at a description of the second coming of Jesus Christ?

According to Joel 3:12, at what location will the fighting end?

What will the world see when Christ returns (see Matthew 24:29-31)?

Where will Christ make His victorious ascent, according to Zechariah 14:4?

Charting What We've Learned

Now look at the map on page 69. Using the numbers on the map, follow the progression of the campaign at Armageddon, matching each number on the map with its corresponding number in the list titled "The Eight Stages."

Next, read the following verses, which are in *mixed order* (these are the same verses you just read to answer the questions earlier in this lesson). Write these verse references in the *proper* locations on the map (for example, write "Revelation 16:12-16" at location #1 on the map).

Micah 2:12

Isaiah 34:1-8

Zechariah 14:4

Revelation 18:10,17,19

Joel 3:12

Zechariah 12:10

Revelation 16:12-16

Zechariah 14:2

A Remarkable Truth

Can you imagine all the manpower, all the strategies, all the work that will go into the Antichrist's efforts to bring all the great armies of the world to Armageddon? And behind the scenes, it's actually *God* who will orchestrate every detail of the event. Proverbs 21:1 tells us, "The king's heart is like channels of water in the hand of the LORD; He turns it wherever He wishes." Though at first it may not seem like it, God will be in full control of all that happens. And in the end, He will turn the Battle of Armageddon to His advantage for a clear and dramatic victory over all the forces of Antichrist.

The God who is totally sovereign over the future is the same God who cares about you and knows your personal future. Is there anything in your future that you are worried about? Give your concerns to Him in prayer...right now. Why hold your problems in your hands when you can place them in His hands?

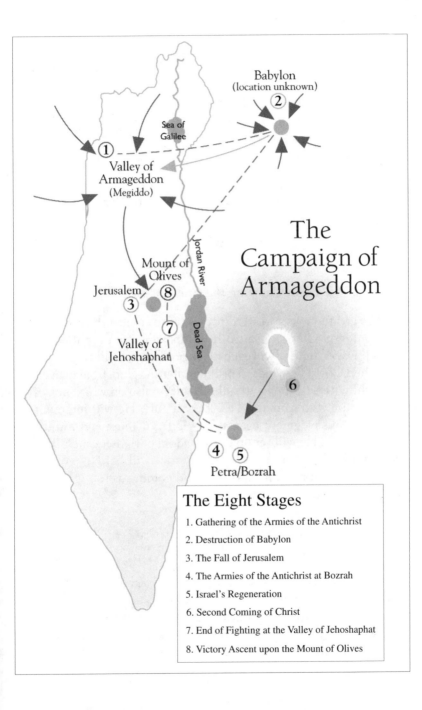

Babylon
(location unknown)
②

Sea of
Galilee

①
Valley of
Armageddon
(Megiddo)

Jordan River

Mount of
Olives
Jerusalem ⑧
③

Valley of
Jehoshaphat

Dead Sea

⑦

6

④ ⑤
Petra/Bozrah

The Campaign of Armageddon

The Eight Stages

1. Gathering of the Armies of the Antichrist
2. Destruction of Babylon
3. The Fall of Jerusalem
4. The Armies of the Antichrist at Bozrah
5. Israel's Regeneration
6. Second Coming of Christ
7. End of Fighting at the Valley of Jehoshaphat
8. Victory Ascent upon the Mount of Olives

Lesson 14

THE GLORIOUS APPEARING

See pages 65–66 in *Charting the End Times*.

The greatest event in all history is yet to come—the return of the Lord Jesus Christ to earth! It is impossible for us to imagine the fullness of all that will take place on that incredibly glorious day, when Christ descends in brilliant, blazing glory from heaven on a white horse, along with all the saints, also on white horses and wearing white linen robes. In holy fury, He will mete out instantaneous judgment against all God's enemies, and in ultimate triumph, He will set up His kingdom of righteousness, justice, and love. What an exciting day that will be! No wonder the apostle Paul referred to the second coming as the "glorious appearing" (Titus 2:13 KJV).

Getting a Clear Picture of the Glorious Appearing

The Bible has at least 325 prophecies about the second coming. We believe one of the best ways to appreciate the significance of Christ's return is to read the Scriptures themselves and see what they say. Read the following questions and Bible passages, and write what they tell us:

When will the glorious appearing take place (Matthew 24:29)?

What miraculous signs will occur at this time (Matthew 24:29)?

What will the people on earth see, and how will they respond (Matthew 24:30)?

How will Christ appear (Revelation 19:11-13)?

Who will be with Christ (Jude 14; Revelation 19:14)?

What will Christ be prepared to do (Jude 15; Revelation 19:15a)?

Where will Christ descend (Zechariah 14:4)?

With whom will Christ do battle (Revelation 19:19)?

What will happen in that battle (Revelation 19:20-21)?

What will then happen to Satan (Revelation 20:1-3)?

Who will reign with Christ, and how long will this reign
continue (Revelation 20:4)?

Giving Proper Honor to Jesus Christ

Titles and names can tell us a lot about a person. Read Revelation 19:11-21, and write the five titles used in this passage for the Lord Jesus Christ.

1.

2.

3.

4.

5.

Taking the Glorious Appearing to Heart

Are you living in anticipation of Christ's return? We are! Try to think of at least three reasons to look forward to our Lord's second coming, and write them below. Let these reasons serve as reminders of the wonderful future ahead of you!

1.

2.

3.

Lesson 15

THE 75-DAY INTERVAL

See pages 66–67 in *Charting the End Times*.

The Bible appears to tell us that the change from the end of the Tribulation—which will be marked by great destruction—over to the glorious Millennial kingdom of Christ will not be instantaneous. Rather, we'll go through a time of transition, a time in which the Lord Jesus Christ prepares the earth for His new kingdom.

While this transition period may not seem all that significant, it's important to understand, for it helps to explain the different "numbers of days" that Scripture gives in relation to the end times. Some people point to these differences and wonder if the Bible has contradictions or is incorrect, but if we look at these numbers carefully, we can figure out how they work together and how they, in fact, are not contradictory.

As we study this 75-day interval, you'll want to look at the chart on page 77. You'll find this chart helpful as you attempt to follow the different Scripture passages we read.

The Number of Days in the Tribulation

From the beginning of the Tribulation to the midpoint, two special witnesses will prophesy about God. How many days will they continue their ministry, according to Revelation

11:3? (Note: This number of days is the same as 42 months, or three-and-a-half years.)

From the midpoint of the Tribulation to the end, the people of Israel will flee into the wilderness to hide from Antichrist. How many days will they stay in this "place prepared of God"?

And during this same time, for how many months will Antichrist blaspheme God (see Revelation 13:5-6)?

Doing the Math

From the beginning of the Tribulation to the midpoint we have 1260 days, or 42 months, or three-and-a-half years. And from the midpoint to the end, we have 1260 days, or 42 months, or three-and-a-half years. The length of the entire Tribulation, then, is seven years, which fits with what Daniel said about the Tribulation lasting for what we would call "one week of years," or seven years (Daniel 9:27).

On the chart on page 77, you'll see that from the midpoint of the Tribulation to the second coming, there are 1260 days.

Now let's read Daniel 12:11-12 (KJV):

> From the time that the daily sacrifice shall be taken away, and the abomination that maketh desolate set up, there shall be a thousand two hundred and ninety days. Blessed is he that waiteth, and cometh to the thousand three hundred and five and thirty days.

In those verses, Daniel mentions a point at which 1290 days will be reached (which is *30 days* beyond the 1260 days in the last half of the Tribulation), and then another point at which 1335 days will be reached (which is *75 days* beyond the 1260 days).

Setting Up the Millennial Temple

Notice that Daniel 12:11 mentions the abomination of desolation that takes place in the Temple at the midpoint of the Tribulation. Because the focus is the Temple, we can safely assume that the 30-day interval relates to the Temple. What's more, the prophet Ezekiel describes the features of the Millennial Temple in Ezekiel 40–48. It's very likely, then, that the first 30 days after the end of the Tribulation will be used to set up the Millennial Temple and prepare it for use.

Blessing Upon Those Who Enter the Millennial Kingdom

Next, in Daniel 12:12, we are told that those who make it to day 1335 are "blessed." This is probably a reference to the people in Matthew 25:34: "Then shall the King say unto them on his right hand, Come, ye blessed of my Father, inherit the kingdom prepared for you from the foundation of the world" (KJV).

The clues in Daniel 12:11-12 lead us to believe the 75-day interval is a time of preparation for the kingdom. We need to remember that much of the world will have been destroyed during the Tribulation, making it necessary for our Lord to do some renovation work before He brings us into His Millennial kingdom.

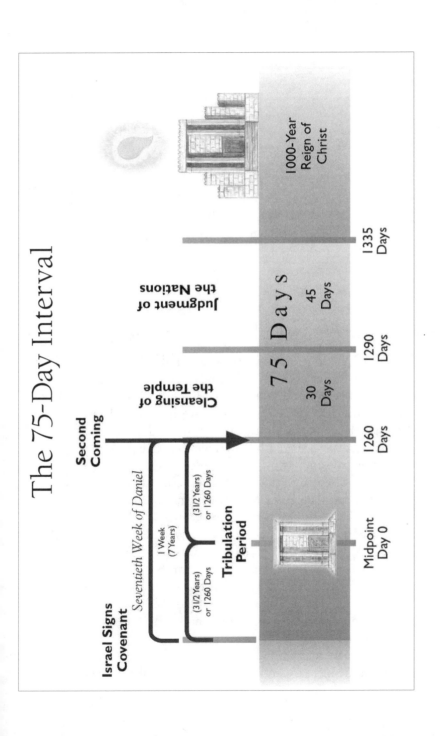

The 75-Day Interval

Israel Signs Covenant

Second Coming

Seventieth Week of Daniel

1 Week (7 Years)

(3 1/2 Years) or 1260 Days

(3 1/2 Years) or 1260 Days

Tribulation Period

Midpoint Day 0

Cleansing of the Temple

Judgment of the Nations

7 5 D a y s

30 Days

45 Days

1000-Year Reign of Christ

1260 Days

1290 Days

1335 Days

Lesson 16

THE MILLENNIUM, PART 1

See pages 70–72 in *Charting the End Times*.

From the time of the very earliest civilizations, our world has known conflict and wars. There has never been an extended period of true peace at any one time all over the globe. Even during the times when weapons have been set aside, there has been verbal, emotional, and political discord and hatred between people groups. Man, with his sin nature, is simply not capable of bringing true and lasting peace to this world.

Only when the Prince of Peace, Jesus Christ, comes to the world and sets up His kingdom will there be real harmony and peace. He is the only one who has the power and ability to enforce the peace, righteousness, and abundance that will mark the 1000-year earthly utopia known as the Millennial kingdom.

The word *millennium* is a Latin term that means "a thousand years." In the Bible, we read that the kingdom set up by Christ after the end of the Tribulation will last 1000 years (Revelation 20:4). In addition, this kingdom marks the transition between history and eternity.

There are many Bible passages that describe for us what this future time of peace and prosperity will be like. In fact, there is so much to learn that we'll study the Millennium in both this lesson and the next.

First Things First

The problems in our world all got their start on that day when Satan tempted Adam and Eve to disobey God in the Garden of Eden. Since that time, Satan has been "as a roaring lion…seeking whom he may devour" (1 Peter 5:8 KJV). He is "the god of this world," who has "blinded the minds of the unbelieving" (2 Corinthians 4:4).

According to Revelation 20:1-3, what will happen to Satan at the beginning of the Millennial kingdom?

Why will this happen (verse 3)?

What effect do you think this will have on the earth?

A Description of the Millennial Kingdom

The Ruler

Who will rule this kingdom (see Revelation 20:4)?

What five titles are given to Christ in this kingdom (Isaiah 9:6)?

What does Isaiah 9:7 say about the government in this kingdom?

How many times does Revelation 20:1-7 mention the number of years that the kingdom will last?

The Homage

The prophet Zechariah had much to say about Christ's coming kingdom. Read Zechariah 14:9,16-21 and answer the following questions:

How widespread is this kingdom, according to verse 9?

What will the inhabitants of this kingdom do each year (verse 16)?

What will happen if they don't do this (verses 17-19)?

The Inhabitants

Isaiah also describes for us this coming kingdom. Read Isaiah 65:19-25 and answer the following:

What does verse 20 tell us about the ages of people?

What do verses 21-22 tell us about the living conditions of that era?

According to verse 25, what will conditions be like in the animal world?

Now read Isaiah 65:19-25, and write four or five things that will *not* exist in Christ's future kingdom.

1.

2.

3.

4.

5.

Based on what you've learned from Zechariah 14 and Isaiah 65, what will set Christ's Millennial kingdom apart from the imperfect kingdoms of men?

An Appropriate Response

Through this lesson, we've gotten some idea of what Christ's glorious kingdom will be like. When was the last time you thanked God for the gifts that are waiting for you in the future? Take a few moments now to tell Him what you're looking forward to, and to thank Him for His gracious provision.

Lesson 17

THE MILLENNIUM, PART 2

See pages 70–72 in *Charting the End Times*.

The Millennium will be an incredible time unlike any the world has ever known. The Adamic curse will be rolled back, people will live for 1000 years, and the Lord Jesus Christ will rule the world with perfect peace, justice, and righteousness. What's more, the great blessings promised by the Old Testament prophets to the nation of Israel will come to fruition, and the surrounding Gentile nations will benefit from the overflow of those blessings. No longer will Israel be scorned and her people persecuted. Instead, the multitudes of the world will come to Jerusalem to worship Christ, and Israel will be fully restored and made the center of Christ's kingdom.

Just how different will the Millennial kingdom be? Scripture gives us some glimpses of the wonders to come; let's look at them.

The People in the Kingdom

Read Zephaniah 3:9-20, and write down your answers to the following questions.

According to verse 9, what will all the people do?

What attitude marks the people described in verse 12?

What will be true about the people of Israel, according to verse 13?

What will the Lord remove (see verse 15)?

Write at least seven different things the Lord will do, according to verses 17-20.

1.

2.

3.

4.

5.

6.

7.

The Environment of the Kingdom

What will happen to the land and animals, according to Isaiah 35:1-2?

Isaiah 30:23-24?

Isaiah 11:6-7?

The Spiritual Aspect of the Kingdom

What does Isaiah 11:9 say about the people of the earth?

What does Jeremiah 32:37-40 say about the people of Israel?

What will the nations do, according to Isaiah 2:2-3?

What promise is given in Isaiah 59:21?

The End of the Kingdom

As we learned earlier, the kingdom will last for 1000 years. The fact that Revelation 20:1-7 says this six different times strongly supports that the Bible is talking about a *literal* future kingdom, and not just a symbolic event or time period.

We learned earlier that those believers who survive to the end of the Tribulation will go straight into the Millennial kingdom. Because they were not raptured, they will not have glorified bodies. These believers will be able to give birth to children (which explains the infants and children mentioned in Isaiah 11:6-7 and 65:20). These "kingdom children" will have the opportunity to choose between following Christ and rebelling against Him.

It is these children whom Satan will attempt to lure in his final rebellion, which will take place at the end of the Millennium.

When will Satan be released, according to Revelation 20:7?

What will he do when he is released (verse 8)?

How will God respond (verse 9)?

What will then happen to Satan, and who else will face the same fate (verse 10)?

Charting What We've Learned

On page 87 is a chart depicting the Millennium. Below are listed some Bible passages. Read the following questions, and write each of the following Bible passages in the correct location on the chart.

What part of the chart does Jeremiah 33:17 speak about?

What part of the chart is mentioned in Revelation 20:7?

Where would you place Matthew 24:29-30 on the chart?

And where would you place Revelation 20:1-4?

Key Events of the Millennium

Christ's Second Coming

Beginning of Millennium

Christ on Davidic Throne

Removal of the Curse

Millennial Temple

Temple Sacrifices

End of Millennium

Satan's Last Revolt

Great White Throne Judgment

Eternity

75-Day Interval

1000 Years

Lesson 18

THE GREAT WHITE THRONE JUDGMENT

See pages 72–74 in *Charting the End Times*.

Through the ages, people have gone to great lengths to deny that they will one day be judged by the Lord. Some individuals who shudder at the prospect of facing God in judgment go so far as to refuse to acknowledge His existence or their accountability to Him. But no matter what people may try to do, they cannot escape the intuitive sense that there really will come a day of judgment. Their disbelief will never negate the biblical truth that after death comes judgment: "It is appointed unto men once to die, but after this the judgment" (Hebrews 9:27).

The Great White Throne Judgment is not the same event as the Judgment Seat of Christ. The latter will take place immediately after the Rapture, and is a time of judgment for believers and the giving out of their rewards. The Great White Throne Judgment will take place at the end of the Millennial reign and is the final judgment for people of *all* ages who rejected God during their time on earth.

A Preview of the Judgment

This judgment is graphically described in Revelation 20:11-15. Read this passage, and answer the following:

What words are used to describe "the dead" who are standing before the throne of judgment (verse 12)?

Read verses 12 and 15. What kind of books are used for this judgment?

What are these people judged "according to" (see verses 12b and 13b)?

What does verse 13 tell us about the scope of this judgment?

What is the final destination of those not found written in the book mentioned in verse 15?

The Particulars of the Judgment

The Judge

The Great White Throne Judgment is not great because of the size of it or the great number of people who stand before it, but because of the greatness of the one who sits upon the throne.

Whom does John 5:22 identify as the Judge?

What does Hebrews 4:13 tell us about this Judge?

According to 1 Peter 2:22, why is Jesus the only one who can possibly judge the world "in righteousness"?

The People

What does John 5:28-29 say will call the dead out of their graves?

From where will the dead come, according to Revelation 20:13?

According to Philippians 2:10-11, what will the people at this judgment do?

The Books

What two kinds of books are mentioned in Revelation 20:12?

How will the dead be judged, according to verses 12-13?

What specific book is mentioned in Revelation 20:15? What will happen to those whose names are *not* found in it?

What does this tell us about the destination of those whose names *are* found in the book?

The Place

The Great White Throne Judgment will end with the partici-pants being "thrown into the lake of fire" (Revelation 20:15). Write what you learn about the lake of fire from the following verses:

Matthew 25:41—

Mark 9:43-44—

Revelation 21:8—

According to Matthew 25:41,46, how long will this punishment last?

Warning Others of the Judgment

It's very sobering to think that the consequences of rejecting Christ will last forever. Those who refuse Christ as their Savior will experience eternal separation from God, eternal darkness, eternal punishment. The torment described in the Bible is very real (see Luke 16:24) and permanent (see Luke 16:26).

Have you thought about your unsaved family members, friends, and coworkers in this light? Do you feel a greater compassion for them when you consider their eventual destiny? What actions can you take in the days ahead to make a difference?

The Great White Throne Judgment

Great White Throne

Jn 5:22

Books of Man's Works
Rev 20:12-13

Lamb's Book of Life
Rev 21:27

Law
Gal 3:20

The Book of Life
Rev 20:15

Sheol—Hades

Former Paradise

Great Gulf

Torment—Lk 16:18-31

Prison of Fallen Angels—2 Pet 2:4; Jude 6

Lake of Fire

Lesson 19

THE ETERNAL STATE

See pages 75–77 in *Charting the End Times*.

There are some places on earth that are called *paradise* because of their exceptional beauty, their year-around pleasant weather, and the unusual variety of recreational opportunities they offer. Such places are usually considered ideal vacation spots—places that tourists look forward to visiting with great anticipation.

There's one paradise that far exceeds any ever known by man, and that's our future home in heaven. We're given a brief but majestic glimpse into heaven in the final two chapters of the Bible—Revelation 21–22. And what we find there is so amazing that it's beyond comprehension.

The apostle John pulls the curtain back for us by beginning his description of heaven with these words:

> I saw a new heaven and a new earth; for the first heaven and the first earth passed away, and there is no more sea. And I saw the holy city, new Jerusalem, coming down out of heaven from God, made ready as a bride adorned for her husband. And I heard a loud voice from the throne, saying, Behold, the tabernacle of God is among men, and he will dwell among them,

and they shall be his people, and God himself shall be
among them, and God shall wipe away every tear from
their eyes; and there will no longer be any death; there
will no longer be any mourning, or crying, or pain; for
the first things have passed away (Revelation 21:1-4).

Keep in mind that God planned this wonderful place for you
and me even before He created the earth (see Ephesians 1:3-4)!
And the best part of all this is that God will dwell with us. He will
be in our midst. We will have direct fellowship with Him and walk
in the light of His presence (Revelation 21:23).

Specifics About Heaven

What's particularly notable about heaven is not what we will
find there, but what we *won't* find there. Read the following verses,
and write what is lacking in heaven:

21:1—

21:4—

21:8—

21:22—

21:23—

21:25—

21:27—

22:2—

22:3—

Benefits We Will Enjoy in Heaven

Now let's consider some of the wonderful *benefits* of heaven! Read the verses below, and write what we as God's children will enjoy:

21:3—eternal fellowship with _____

21:4—eternal freedom from _____

21:5—our thirst eternally fulfilled by _____

22:2—eternal fruit from _____

22:3—eternal opportunities to serve _____

22:5—an eternal reign with _____

Physical Characteristics of the New Jerusalem

Next, read the physical description of the New Jerusalem in Revelation 21:10-27. What does this description tell you about the city?

Waiting with Great Anticipation

What do you look forward to the most about heaven? For some of us, it's being reunited with loved ones. For others, it's the permanent freedom we'll know from the effects of sin. For still others, it's a time when we will know true joy and perfection, instead of sorrow and imperfections. There are many reasons to long for heaven.

Yet so often, it's easy for us to become ensnared by the day-to-day routines and obligations of life that we always have our eyes focused on that which is earthly and temporal rather than that which is heavenly and eternal. Are you going through life looking down at the earth, or are you looking upward in anticipation of heaven? The great Puritan pastor and writer Matthew Henry encouraged us to do the latter when he wrote: "Our duty as Christians is always to keep heaven in our eye and earth under our feet."

Won't you make that your commitment...today and *always?*

Lesson 20

THE DISPENSATIONS

See pages 81–83 in *Charting the End Times*.

Through the ages, God's plan for mankind has unfolded in stages. With each stage or dispensation, He has revealed more and more information about the present time and the future.

The English word *dispensation* translates the Greek noun *oikonoma*, often rendered "administration" in modern Bible translations. A dispensation, then, is a distinct administration in the development of God's plan for human history. The apostle Paul spoke of dispensations in Ephesians 3:2 ("Ye have heard of the dispensation of the grace of God which is given me to you-ward" [KJV]) and Colossians 1:25-26 ("I am made a minister, according to the dispensation of God which is given to me for you, to fulfill the word of God" [KJV]).

While God works in human history in distinct, identifiable stages, the principles of God's plan of redemption have always remained constant. Salvation has always been by grace through faith. For those who lived before Christ's death on the cross, faith anticipated the eventual fulfillment of the promise of salvation. And for all people from the time of the cross onward, faith looks back to the finished work of Christ on the cross.

The three basic principles of dispensationalism (or dispensational theology) are:

- consistently interpreting the Bible in a plain, literal sense

- recognizing that God has a plan for national Israel that is distinct from the church

- acknowledging that the ultimate goal of history is the glorification of God

Identifying the Stages of History

On page 100 is a chart that depicts the seven stages of history, or the seven dispensations. In each stage, man has certain responsibilities to fulfill to God. Read the verses below, and write down the responsibilities involved in each dispensation:

The Dispensation of Innocence—The shortest of the dispensations, which ended with Adam and Eve's fall into sin. Genesis 2:15-17—

The Dispensation of Conscience—This describes the period between the Fall and the Flood. Genesis 4:4—

The Dispensation of Human Government—After the Flood, God said He would not directly judge men until the second coming. From the post-Flood days onward, a human agency known as civil government was established by God for the purpose of mediating judgment and restraining the evil of men. Genesis 8:15; 9:7—

The Dispensations

Eternity Past

Eternity Future — Great White Throne

	Creation / Innocence	The Fall / Conscience	The Flood / Human Government	Tower of Babel / Promise	Exodus / Law	Church Age	Millennial Reign
Responsibility	Obey God Gen 1:26-28; 2:15-17	Do Good, Blood Sacrifice Gen 3:5, 7, 22; 4:4	Scatter and Multiply Gen 8:15-9:7	Dwell in Canaan Gen 12:1-7	Keep the Whole Law Exod 19:3-8	Faith in Jesus, Keep Doctrine Pure Jn 1:12; Rom 8:1-4; Eph 2:8-9	Obey and Worship Jesus Isa 11:3-5; Zech 14:9,16
Failure	Disobedience Gen 3:1-6	Wickedness Gen 6:5-6, 11-12	Did Not Scatter Gen 11:1-4	Dwelt in Egypt Gen 12:10; 46:6	Broke Law 2 Kgs 17:7-20; Mt 27:1-25	Impure Doctrine Jn 5:39-40; 2 Tim 3:1-7	Final Rebellion Rev 20:7-9
Judgment	Curse and Death Gen 3:7-19	Flood Gen 6:7, 13; 7:11-14	Confusion of Languages Gen 11:5-9	Egyptian Bondage Exod 1:8-14	Worldwide Dispersion Deut 28:63-66; Lk 21:20-24	Apostasy, False Doctrine 2 Ths 2:3; 2 Tim 4:3	Satan Loosed, Eternal Hell Rev 20:11-15

Israel

Dispersion of Israel Ezk 36:16-19

Regathering of Israel Ezk 36:20-24

Church Age Ezk 36:16-19

Law Fulfilled Mt 27:50-51

Rapture of Saved 1 Ths 4:16-17

Return of Christ in Glory Rev 19:11-16

7 Years Tribulation

Armageddon

Lake of Fire

Biblical Dispensations

The Dispensation of Promise—This period is marked by God's call of Abram (Abraham) and God's promise to him and his descendants, both spiritual and physical. Genesis 12:1-3—

The Dispensation of Law/Israel—God never intended for Israel to be saved by keeping the Law. Rather, the purpose of the Law was to show the people how to live. It was a temporary instrument that would point to their need for salvation through Christ. Genesis 19:5-8—

The Dispensation of Grace (Church Age)—Through the church, God's grace is extended to everyone worldwide through the gospel. John 1:12; Ephesians 2:8-9—

The Dispensation of the Millennial Kingdom—During Christ's 1000-year reign, the promises God made to Israel will be fulfilled to Israel as a nation, and the church will rule with Christ as His bride. Zechariah 14:9,16—

The Church and Israel Are Separate Entities in God's Plan

When we properly recognize the stages through which God's plan unfolds, we will have a correct understanding of God's prophetic timetable for history. From the time of Abraham to Christ's death on the cross, God's plan was for Himself to be made manifest to the world through Israel. But Israel turned from God, and God is now working through the church to make Himself known to the world. We are now living in the church age, or what is known as the age of grace, which is the period *between* the first 69 weeks of Daniel's 70-weeks prophecy and the 70th week. After the church is raptured, God will once again work through the nation of Israel (as evident by the 144,000 Jewish witnesses in Revelation 7 and the two Jewish witnesses in Revelation 11) and fulfill His Old Testament promises to Israel. Thus, the doctrine of the pretribulational Rapture of the church is closely identified with dispensationalism.

All to the Glory of God

As mentioned earlier, through the ages, God has unveiled His eternal plan in stages, and the end purpose of everything is for God to be glorified. Though each of us is just one very small part of a very large plan, still, every single one of us can make an important contribution to glorifying God. In Matthew 5:16, Jesus said, "Let your light so shine before men, that they may see your good works, and glorify your Father which is in heaven" (KJV). And in 1 Corinthians 10:31, the apostle Paul wrote, "Whether therefore ye eat, or drink, or whatsoever ye do, do all to the glory of God" (KJV).

Are you living today to the glory of God? Would those who hear your words and see your actions be able to see God through them?

What are some practical ways you can bring glory to God through…

Your words?

Your interaction with your spouse (or a family member)?

Your interaction with your children (or a friend)?

Your work?

After you finish writing your answers, take a moment to pray to the Lord, and ask Him to enable you to become one who contributes to glorifying Him before a watching world.

Lesson 21

THE 70 WEEKS OF DANIEL

See pages 89–90 in *Charting the End Times*.

Daniel's "70 weeks" prophecy, given in Daniel 9:24-27, is extremely important to a clear understanding of Bible prophecy. In this prophecy, we can see that God has not replaced Israel with the church, but rather, that there is coming a day when God will once again work through the nation of Israel. In the first 69 weeks of the prophecy, the focal point is the nation of Israel, and in the 70th week, the focal point again is Israel. What's key is understanding the gap between the 69th and 70th week, as well as what will happen during the 70th week.

Daniel 9:27 describes for us the events of the 70th week:

> He shall confirm the covenant with many for one week: and in the midst of the week he shall cause the sacrifice and the oblation to cease, and for the overspreading of abominations he shall make it desolate, even until the consummation, and that determined shall be poured upon the desolate (KJV).

In 2 Thessalonians 2:3-4, we read that the abomination of desolation will be committed by "that man of sin...the son of perdition" (KJV), which is a reference to the Antichrist. Because we know that each week in Daniel's prophecy refers to a week of years, or seven years, we know that in the middle of a seven-year period, the Antichrist will desecrate the Temple. This is a still-future event that will take place during the seven-year Tribulation.

Using Math to Understand the "70 Weeks" Prophecy

Keep in mind that each week represents seven years:

69 x 7 x 360 = 173,880 days

March 5, 444 B.C. + 173,880 = March 30, A.D. 33

Verification

444 B.C. to A.D. 33 = 476 years

476 years x 365.2421989 days = 173,855 days

+ days between March 5 and March 30 = 25 days

Total = 173,880 days

Rationale for 360-Day Years

½ week—Daniel 9:27

Time, times, and half a time—Daniel 7:25; 12:7; Revelation 12:14

1260 days—Revelation 11:3; 12:6

42 months—Revelation 11:2; 13:5

Thus 42 months = 1260 days = time, times, and half a time = ½ week

Therefore: month = 30 days; year = 360 days[*]

The Breakdown of the 70 Weeks of Daniel

On pages 106-7 is a chart that lays out the details of Daniel's "70 weeks" prophecy. Using the chart, answer these questions:

---

[*] Harold Hoebner, *Chronological Aspects of the Life of Christ* (Grand Rapids: Zondervan, 1977), p. 139.

The 70 Weeks

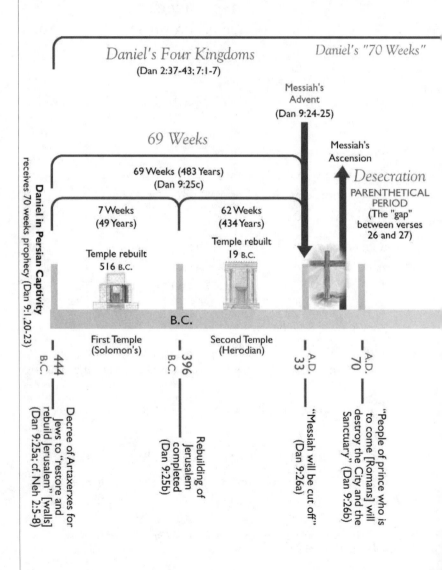

Daniel's Four Kingdoms (Dan 2:37-43; 7:1-7)

Daniel's "70 Weeks"

Messiah's Advent (Dan 9:24-25)

Messiah's Ascension

Desecration

PARENTHETICAL PERIOD (The "gap" between verses 26 and 27)

69 Weeks

69 Weeks (483 Years) (Dan 9:25c)

7 Weeks (49 Years)

62 Weeks (434 Years)

Temple rebuilt 516 B.C.

Temple rebuilt 19 B.C.

Daniel in Persian Captivity receives 70 weeks prophecy (Dan 9:1,20-23)

B.C.

First Temple (Solomon's)

Second Temple (Herodian)

444 B.C.

396 B.C.

A.D. 33

A.D. 70

Decree of Artaxerxes for Jews to "restore and rebuild Jerusalem" [walls] (Dan 9:25a; cf. Neh 2:5-8)

Rebuilding of Jerusalem completed (Dan 9:25b)

"Messiah will be cut off" (Dan 9:26a)

"People of prince who is to come [Romans] will destroy the City and the Sanctuary" (Dan 9:26b)

# of Daniel

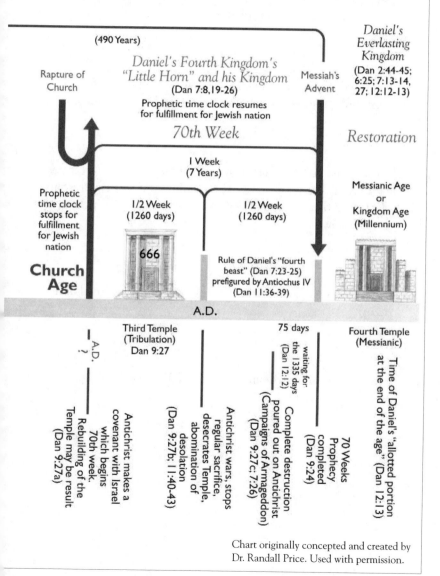

Chart originally concepted and created by
Dr. Randall Price. Used with permission.

What event in 444 B.C. initiates the beginning of the 70 weeks of Daniel?

What event in 396 B.C. marks the completion of the first 7 weeks of the 70-week prophecy?

What event in A.D. 33 marks the completion of the first 69 weeks of Daniel's 70-week prophecy (see Daniel 9:26a)?

In the center of the chart is what's labeled as the "Parenthetical Period." What does the chart tell us about this period in relation to the Jewish nation? What age is this Parenthetical Period known as?

What event marks the *beginning* of the 70th week (see Daniel 9:27a)?

What event marks the *middle* of the 70th week (see Daniel 9:27; 11:40-43)?

What event marks the *end* of the 70th week (hint: look near the top of the chart, along the vertical line that marks the completion of the 70th week)?

How many Temples are featured on this chart, and what is each one called?

What the 70 Weeks of Daniel Means to Us Today

While there's more we can learn about the 70 weeks of Daniel, we've examined the most important aspect of this prophecy: the basic outline of the 70 weeks and what they involve. The pattern set for us in Jesus' Olivet Discourse and Revelation chapters 4–19 confirms that Daniel's 70th week is still in the future. There really is coming a time when God will work once again through the nation of Israel, as affirmed by Romans 11:25-26:

> I would not, brethren, that ye should be ignorant of this mystery, lest ye should be wise in your own conceits; that blindness in part is happened to Israel, until the fullness of the Gentiles [the church age] be come in. And so all Israel shall be saved: as it is written, There shall come out of Zion the Deliverer, and shall turn away ungodliness from Jacob (KJV).

Many of the promises God made to Israel in the Old Testament have not yet been fulfilled. Some people believe those promises now belong to the church. But if that were the case, then God has failed to keep His promises to Israel. His promises were clearly directed at the nation—not some other body of people.

We can rest assured that God will carry out His promises exactly as He said He would. Israel's disobedience has not thwarted His original plans. Israel will come back to God someday, exactly as the Bible predicts. This fact helps us to know that we can trust God to fulfill every single one of the promises He has given us!

Lesson 22

THE VARIOUS VIEWS OF THE RAPTURE

See pages 106–8 in *Charting the End Times*.

The vast majority of Christians who interpret the Bible literally agree that one day, we will be raptured. But not all of them agree on the *timing* of the Rapture. Part of the problem is that we cannot point to just one verse and say, "This is when the Rapture will happen." Rather, we need to bring together several different passages and come to a conclusion based on careful deduction.

There are four views on the timing of the Rapture:

1. *The Pre-Tribulation View*—the Rapture will happen before the Tribulation, sparing the church from the outpouring of God's wrath.

2. *The Partial Rapture View*—Christ will rapture only those who "look for him" (Hebrews 9:28), leaving others to be raptured at another time. This view is not popular for many reasons, including the fact that it's not supported by rapture teachings in the Scriptures.

3. *The Mid-Tribulation View*—Christ will rapture all Christians in the middle of the Tribulation. The two witnesses in Revelation 11 are believed to illustrate the Rapture, but the problem here is that the two witnesses are *Jewish*

individuals who minister to Jews in Jerusalem. Thus, they are not representative of the *church*. The apostle John, who is taken up to heaven in Revelation 4:1-3 at the beginning of the Tribulation, is a more appropriate representative of the church.

4. *The Post-Tribulation View*—The church will go through the Tribulation and be raptured just before Christ returns. Thus those who are raptured will go up to the sky, then come right back down, allowing no time for the judgment of believers' works and the Marriage Supper of the Lamb.

Comparing the Views

The three major views related to the timing of the Rapture are the pre-Trib, mid-Trib, and post-Trib views. Let's consider the pre-Trib view in the light of Scripture, and write down our findings.

The Promise

What promise does Jesus Christ give to the church in Revelation 3:10?

Some people say this promise was given to the church at Philadelphia because it appears in the context of a letter written to the church in that Asian city. However, we can be certain the passage applies to the church in general for these reasons:

1) the verse refers to a future event

2) the church in Philadelphia no longer exists

3) this was a letter to all the churches

4) the verse explicitly states this promise cannot be fulfilled until a time of trial "which shall come upon *all* the world" (KJV), not just the church at Philadelphia

An Unknowable Fact

What does Matthew 24:42 say about the Lord's coming?

What does Matthew 24:44 say about the Lord's coming?

The fact that both Matthew 24:42 and 44 assert it's impossible to know the time of Christ's coming tells us there are no clues by which we can calculate the timing of His appearance. If the Rapture were to happen at the *end* of the Tribulation, then Matthew 24:42,44 would no longer be true, for all we need to know is the time the Tribulation began, and we would be able to calculate the date of Christ's return seven years later. But if the Rapture happens at the *beginning* of the Tribulation, then we truly would have no way of knowing the timing.

The fact that we do not know the timing of the Rapture is referred to as *imminency*—in other words, the Rapture is something that could take place at any time.

Rescued from What?

What promise do we find in 1 Thessalonians 1:10?
(Keep in mind that the context of 1 Thessalonians 1:10 is the Rapture, for Paul tells the Thessalonians that the second coming [or glorious appearing] will not happen until after Antichrist appears [2 Thessalonians 2:1-12, note particularly verse 8].)

What statement does Paul make about Christians in
1 Thessalonians 5:9? (Note that 1 Thessalonians 5:9 follows
one of the major rapture passages in the Bible, which is
1 Thessalonians 4:13-18.)

Where Is the Church?

Finally, if you take the time to read Revelation chapters 4–18,
you'll notice the church is not mentioned once during all the
events of the Tribulation. What might that tell us about the
whereabouts of the church during the Tribulation?

And when the church finally does reappear in Revelation 19,
what is she doing?

Charting What We've Learned

The chart on page 114 pictures the four views of the timing of
the Rapture. Write your answers here and on the chart.

Study timeline #1. Which view does this illustrate?

Which view does timeline #2 depict?

What about timeline #3?

And what view does timeline #4 illustrate?

The Various Views of the Rapture

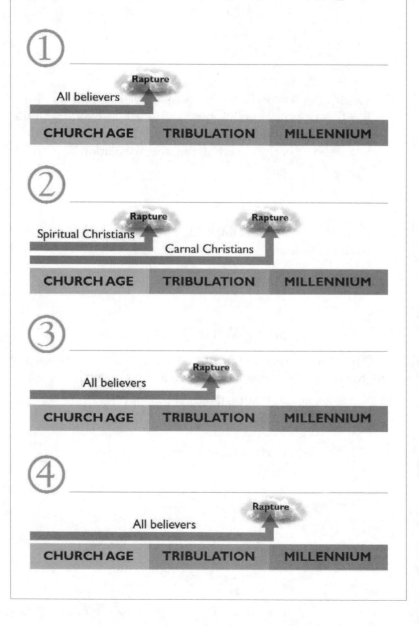

① _____

All believers — **Rapture**

| CHURCH AGE | TRIBULATION | MILLENNIUM |

② _____

Spiritual Christians — **Rapture**

Carnal Christians — **Rapture**

| CHURCH AGE | TRIBULATION | MILLENNIUM |

③ _____

All believers — **Rapture**

| CHURCH AGE | TRIBULATION | MILLENNIUM |

④ _____

All believers — **Rapture**

| CHURCH AGE | TRIBULATION | MILLENNIUM |

Lesson 23

THE TWO PHASES OF HIS COMING

See pages 111–12 in *Charting the End Times*.

If we carefully read all the Scripture passages about Christ's return, we will notice that two different sets of facts emerge from the passages. These differences make it apparent that the second coming occurs in two phases. The appearance of Christ in the air to rapture His church is the first phase, and the second coming, or second phase, will occur at the end of the Tribulation.

There's no doubt there are two phases, for there are multiple passages that describe both. This is not a matter of having just two or three seemingly irreconcilable verses that need to be adjusted so that they fit the other verses. The differences are stark enough that we cannot help but come to the conclusion we're talking about two different events.

On page 117 is a chart that lists more than 20 different rapture passages, and more than 20 different second coming passages.

Observing What Scripture Says

Pick out seven of the rapture passages, and write what they tell you about the Rapture.

1.

2.

3.

4.

5.

6.

7.

Pick out seven of the second coming passages, and write what they tell you about the second coming.

1.

2.

3.

4.

5.

Rapture Passages

John 14:1-3	1 Thessalonians 1:10	Hebrews 9:28
Romans 8:19	1 Thessalonians 2:19	James 5:7-9
1 Corinthians 1:7-8	1 Thessalonians 4:13-18	1 Peter 1:7,13
1 Corinthians 15:51-53	1 Thessalonians 5:9,23	1 Peter 5:4
1 Corinthians 16:22	2 Thessalonians 2:1	1 John 2:28–3:2
Philippians 3:20-21	1 Timothy 6:14	Jude 1:21
Philippians 4:5	2 Timothy 4:1,8	Revelation 2:25
Colossians 3:4	Titus 2:13	

Second Coming Passages

Daniel 2:44-45	Mark 13:14-27	1 Peter 4:12-13
Daniel 7:9-14	Mark 14:62	2 Peter 3:1-14
Daniel 12:1-3	Luke 21:25-28	Jude 1:14-15
Zechariah 12:10	Acts 1:9-11	Revelation 1:7
Zechariah 14:1-15	Acts 3:19-21	Revelation 19:11–20:6
Matthew 13:41	1 Thessalonians 3:13	Revelation 22:7,12,20
Matthew 24:15-31	2 Thessalonians 1:6-10	
Matthew 26:64	2 Thessalonians 2:8	

6.

7.

Based on the sample passages you've read, what differences do you observe between the two events?

Observing the Differences

Now study the chart labeled "The 15 Differences Between the Rapture and the Glorious Appearing" on page 119, and write your observations for the following:

What is the difference between #1 in column one and #1 in column two?

What is the difference between #2 in column one and #2 in column two?

What is the difference between #3 in each column?

Between #4 in each column?

Number 5?

The 15 Differences Between the Rapture and the Glorious Appearing

Rapture / Blessed Hope

1. Christ comes in the air for His own
2. Rapture of all Christians
3. Christians taken to the Father's house
4. No judgment on earth
5. Church taken to heaven
6. Imminent—could happen any moment
7. No signs
8. For believers only
9. Time of joy
10. Before the "day of wrath" (Tribulation)
11. No mention of Satan
12. The judgment seat of Christ
13. Marriage of the Lamb
14. Only His own see Him
15. Tribulation begins

Glorious Appearing

1. Christ comes with His own to earth
2. No one raptured
3. Resurrected saints do not see Father's house
4. Christ judges inhabitants of earth
5. Christ sets up His kingdom on earth
6. Cannot occur for at least 7 years
7. Many signs for Christ's physical coming
8. Affects all humanity
9. Time of mourning
10. Immediately after Tribulation (Matthew 24)
11. Satan bound in abyss for 1000 years
12. No time or place for judgment seat
13. His bride descends with Him
14. Every eye will see Him
15. 1000-year kingdom of Christ begins

Number 6?

Number 7?

Number 8?

Number 9?

Number 10?

Number 11?

Number 12?

Number 13?

Number 14?

Number 15?

Observing the Big Picture: A Worthy Habit

When we write out the facts of Scripture, we cannot help but realize there are a good number of incidents related to Christ's return that simply cannot be reconciled and merged into one event. This affirms the view that there are two phases to Christ's return: First, He will come in the clouds to take Christians home to the Father's house, and second, He will descend upon the Mount of Olives and unleash fiery judgment upon the Antichrist's armies and pave the way to set up His Millennial kingdom here on earth.

Again, there is no one Bible verse that states this in its entirety. That's why it's vital for us to look at Scripture as a whole, and assemble all the information so we can make sense of it. This is a practice we should pursue in relation to any doctrine found in the Bible. Only when we have taken the proper steps in Bible study can we be assured that we will emerge with a clear understanding of what Scripture teaches.

The apostle Paul greatly commended the Christians in the ancient city of Berea because they "examined the Scriptures every day to see if what Paul said was true" (Acts 17:11 NIV). Paul recognized the supremacy of God's Word, and did not mind when his listeners compared his messages to Scripture to make sure his teachings were accurate. Our prayer is that you will be equally zealous in your own pursuit of understanding God's truth, and that you will always let God's Word be the final determiner of what you believe as a Christian!

Lesson 24

THE RESURRECTIONS AND JUDGMENTS IN SCRIPTURE

See pages 121–23 in *Charting the End Times*.

The common perception people have of a single, all-encompassing judgment day is incorrect. There will not be one judgment day, but several, and each judgment has a specific purpose as well as a specific group of participants.

The One Who Made Resurrection Possible

Before we look at the different resurrections and judgments of Scripture, let's look at the one event that made all of this possible: Christ's own resurrection from the dead.

What did Jesus say about Himself in John 11:25?

What did Jesus say would happen to those who believe in Him, according to John 11:25-26?

What promise do we find in John 14:19?

What would be true about Christians if Christ had not risen from the dead (see 1 Corinthians 15:17)?

The Different Resurrections

According to John 5:28-29, there are two basic categories of resurrections. What are they?

Beyond those two categories, there are several resurrections, and they will occur in the following sequence:

1. The resurrection of Jesus Christ as the first fruit of many to be raised (Romans 6:9; 1 Corinthians 15:23; Colossians 1:18; Revelation 1:18)

2. The resurrection of the redeemed at Christ's coming (Daniel 12:2; Luke 14:14; John 5:29; 1 Thessalonians 4:16; Revelation 20:4,6)

   a. Resurrection of the church at the Rapture

   b. Resurrection of Old Testament believers at the second coming (Jews and Gentiles)

    c. Resurrection of the redeemed at the end of the 1000-year Millennial kingdom

3. The resurrection of the unredeemed (Revelation 20:11-14)

The Different Judgments

Judgment of Church-Age Believers

Earlier in our study (on pages 48–52), we looked at the believers' judgment, which takes place in heaven immediately after the Rapture, at the beginning of the Tribulation. The Rapture is a resurrection or translation of all church-age Christians, both dead and alive, for the purpose of judging their works, participating in the Marriage of the Lamb, and preparing for Christ's return to earth at the glorious appearing. This preparation involves clothing all the church-age saints with white robes, which they will wear when they descend from heaven with Christ (Revelation 19:6-14). In fact, these white robes are proof that these believers will already have gone through their evaluation or judgment before the end of the Tribulation.

Judgment of the Nations

When Christ returns at the end of the Tribulation, He will call the unsaved dead out of their graves, as well as the Old Testament believers. We read about this judgment in Matthew 25:31-46.

According to Matthew 25:31, when will this event occur?

Who will stand before Christ (verse 32)?

How will Christ separate the participants (verses 32-33)?

On what basis will Christ make His decisions, according to verses 34-40?

What is the destination of those on Christ's left side (verses 41,46)?

Why (verses 42-45)?

Now, why is it that Christ will judge people based on their works when Ephesians 2:8-9, which says that salvation is by grace alone, says that we cannot be saved through our works?

Salvation is a free gift, and no amount of good works can help us to obtain it. However, Jesus said, "By their fruits ye shall know them" (Matthew 7:20). In other words, our actions will reveal the true condition of our heart. If we have received the Lord's gift of salvation in our heart, it will be evident in the things that we do. If we lack good fruit in our lives, that's evidence we were never saved in the first place.

At the judgment of the nations, all the unbelievers who are alive on the earth will be put to death through Christ's judgment (Revelation 19:15,20-21). Those believers who are still alive—both Jews and Gentiles—will be ushered into the Millennial kingdom. Because they were not raptured, they will not have received their glorified bodies. It is these people who will populate the Millennial kingdom through their children.

The Great White Throne Judgment

This is the final judgment of history, which we examined earlier on pages 88–93. This is the "resurrection of damnation" spoken of in John 5:29. Because these people rejected God and Christ during their lifetimes on earth, they will be judged not on the basis of Christ's work on the cross, but rather, their own works. And because no one can measure up to God's perfect standard of holiness, these people will be condemned to face everlasting punishment.

The Urgency of the Moment

What thoughts go through your mind as you consider family members, friends, or coworkers who are unsaved and thus destined for eternal separation from God?

Are you praying for opportunities to let your light shine to these people? What are some ways that you can make that happen?

In regard to the unsaved people around you, our hope is that your prayer is the same as that of the apostle Paul's in Colossians 4:3-4:

> Pray for us, too, that God may open a door for our message, so that we may proclaim the mystery of Christ.... Pray that I may proclaim it clearly, as I should.

The Coming Judgments

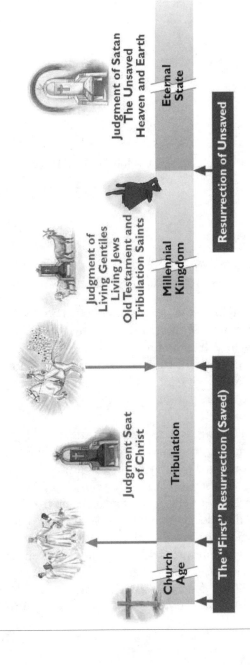

Lesson 25

THE VARIOUS VIEWS OF THE MILLENNIUM

See pages 128–30 in *Charting the End Times*.

The English word *millennium* is based on the Latin term *mille*, which means "one thousand," and the Latin term *annus*, which means "years." It is the Greek term for one thousand (*chilia*) that appears six times in Revelation 20:2-7, defining the length of Christ's earthly kingdom as 1000 years.

Among Christians, there are three different views of the Millennium:

Premillennialism: This view says there will be a future, literal 1000-year reign of Christ upon the earth following our Lord's second coming. That is, Christ will return to earth personally to rule *before* He sets up His 1000-year kingdom. Now, those who hold to premillennialism don't all agree on the timing of the Rapture, but they do agree that Christ will return before the Millennial kingdom begins. What's more, this is the view held by most of those who interpret the Bible conservatively and literally.

Amillennialism: The prefix *a*, in Greek, means "no," so the term *amillennial* means "no thousand years." Amillennialists teach that Christ will not set up a literal, future, 1000-year kingdom on earth. Yet most of them say the kingdom is now present among us in a spiritual form. The proponents of amillennialism say that from the time of Christ's ascension to the time He returns (no Rapture), both good and evil will increase in the world as God's kingdom parallels Satan's kingdom. Then, after Christ returns, there will be a general resurrection and judgment of all people. Thus, all the Bible prophecies related to a coming literal kingdom of Christ are spiritualized in some way, and there is no literal earthly kingdom to speak of.

Postmillennialism: Those who hold to this view say Christ's kingdom is now being extended through the spread of the gospel, and that we are making continual progress to the point that the world will become converted to Christ and, as a result, will become Christianized. Only then will Christ return to the earth. The prefix *post* means "after," so postmillennialism teaches that Christ will return to earth *after* 1000 years have passed.

Postmillennialism also teaches that we are now living in the Millennium, which is not necessarily a literal 1000 years in length. They say that at the end of the Millennium Christ will return, and there will be a general resurrection, the destruction of this creation, and the entry into the eternal state.

Understanding the Definitions

Having read the definitions of the three views as given above, write a very brief description of each view below, using your own words:

Premillennialism:

Amillennialism:

Postmillennialism:

What the Plain Sense of Scripture Tells Us

If you interpret Revelation chapters 19–20 in a literal, plain-sense manner, the only view you can hold to is premillennialism. That's because in Scripture, we see Christ return in Revelation 19, and then we see Him set up His 1000-year kingdom in Revelation 20. Any normal reading of the words and phrases makes it clear that the events of chapter 19 precede the events of chapter 20. That being the case, the second coming precedes the Millennial kingdom, which means the Bible teaches the premillennial view.

Charting What We've Learned

Carefully study the three timelines on page 131. (Note: They do not appear in the same order here as they do in the book *Charting the End Times*.)

Considering the three views of the Millennium, which timeline represents premillennialism?

Which timeline represents postmillennialism?

And which timeline represents amillennialism?

Views of the Millennium

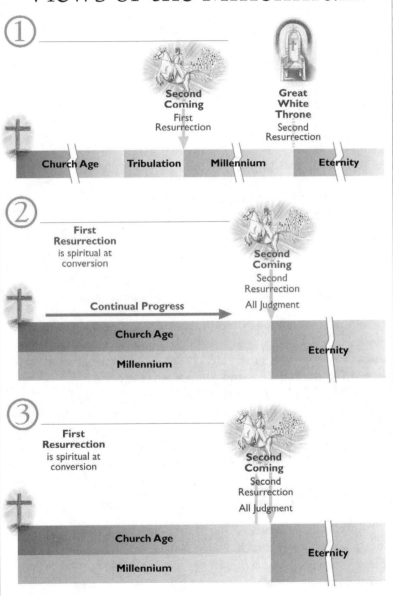

① Second Coming — First Resurrection | Great White Throne — Second Resurrection

Church Age | Tribulation | Millennium | Eternity

② First Resurrection is spiritual at conversion | Second Coming — Second Resurrection — All Judgment

Continual Progress

Church Age

Millennium

Eternity

③ First Resurrection is spiritual at conversion | Second Coming — Second Resurrection — All Judgment

Church Age

Millennium

Eternity

Lesson 26

HISTORY'S END, ETERNITY'S BEGINNING

See pages 134–36 in *Charting the End Times*.

We've covered many topics related to the end times in this study guide. Our hope is that through the study questions, you've come to develop a much clearer understanding of what will happen in the last days, and when it will happen.

We would like to use this final lesson as a "wrap up" that reviews 18 key events mentioned in the last four chapters of the Bible—that is, Revelation chapters 19–22. You can consider this a panoramic overview of what you've learned, which allows you to see how all the pieces of the puzzle fit together.

A Panorama of the Future

Listed below is a breakdown of the verses in Revelation 19–22, along with some related passages. Read each passage, and in the blank space provided, write, in just five or six words, what is happening in that passage.

1. Revelation 19:7-10—

2. Revelation 19:11-18—

3. Revelation 14:14-20; 16:16—

4. Revelation 16:18—

5. Matthew 25:31-46—

6. Revelation 19:20-21—

7. Revelation 20:1-3—

8. Revelation 20:4—

9. Revelation 20:4-6—

10. Revelation 20:7—

11. Revelation 20:8-9—

12. Revelation 20:10—

13. Revelation 20:11-15—

14. Philippians 1:9-11—

15. Revelation 21:1—

16. Revelation 21:2-8—

17. Revelation 21:8–22:5—

18. Revelation 22:6-20—

History's End

Now compare each of the previously mentioned numbers with the corresponding number on the chart on page 135, and see how each event fits into the big picture regarding the future.

A Right Response to God

God has the future planned in great detail, doesn't He? What does this tell you about Him?

What do His plans for heaven and eternity tell you about His love for His children?

Even before Adam and Eve disobeyed God in the Garden of Eden, God already had a plan for man's redemption from sin. He already knew what Jesus would need to accomplish on the cross. And best of all, He already had a wonderful future planned for those who receive Christ as their Savior—a future that is eternal!

If you have trusted Christ as your Savior, you will go to heaven and enjoy everlasting blessings. But if you have not accepted His sacrifice for your sins, then you will be judged according to your works, and be sent to eternal condemnation in the lake of fire.

If you have not yet trusted Jesus to forgive your sin and provide you with eternal life, then we invite you to express your trust in Him right now, with the following prayer:

> Dear God,
>
> Thank You for sending Your Son Jesus to die on the cross for my sins. I confess I am a sinner, and I ask You for Your forgiveness. Today I want to trust Jesus as my Lord and Savior. I give my life and future to You. In Jesus' name I pray, Amen.

Don't miss this great offer of eternal life. After all, that's why Jesus came to earth. He Himself said, "I came that they may have life, and have it more abundantly" (John 10:10). And keep in mind that God "is patient with you, not wanting anyone to perish, but everyone to come to repentance" (2 Peter 3:9 NIV).

And finally, our prayer is that this study guide will spur you to continue studying Bible prophecy, and that it will cause you to "lift up your [head], because your redemption is drawing near" (Luke 21:28 NIV)!

A FINAL WORD

The exciting plan of the ages we have surveyed in this book is not some pipe dream. It is God's own plan, given through the holy men who served Him—the prophets of the Old Testament and the apostles of the New Testament. Bible prophecy is, as we stated earlier, "history written in advance." And just as many prophecies of the past were fulfilled exactly as God predicted and right on time, so will the prophecies about the future—which include His wonderful plan for you—be fulfilled exactly as they are described in Scripture.

We have studied the religions of the world, and no other belief system offers anything that comes close to God's plans for the future. That's why we share them with you—for they will come about! And we don't want you to be left behind when Jesus raptures His church. In fact, we would like to meet you on the way up. But that is up to you, depending on whether or not you have put your trust for eternity in what Jesus did for you on Calvary's cross. Again we say that if there is any doubt about whether you have ever received Him, then ask the resurrected Christ into your heart today. And if you are already a believer, commit yourself to sharing this good news to all you meet.

In anticipation of His return,

Tim LaHaye

Thomas Ice

OTHER PROPHECY BOOKS
BY TIM LAHAYE

Are We Living in the End Times? (Tyndale House)

Charting the End Times (coauthored with Thomas Ice, Harvest House)

The Rapture (Harvest House)

Revelation Unveiled (Zondervan)

The Tim LaHaye Prophecy Study Bible (AMG Publishers)

Understanding Bible Prophecy for Yourself (Harvest House)

PROPHETIC NOVELS COAUTHORED
WITH JERRY B. JENKINS

The Left Behind® Series

Left Behind
Tribulation Force
Nicolae
Soul Harvest
Apollyon
Assassins
The Indwelling
The Mark
Desecration
The Remnant
(four additional books to come)

Left Behind: The Kids®

22 books as of June 2002, with more to come

OTHER PROPHECY BOOKS
BY THOMAS ICE

Charting the End Times (coauthored with Tim LaHaye, Harvest House)

The Great Tribulation, Past or Future? (Kregel)

*The Return: Understanding Christ's Second Coming
and the End Times* (Kregel)

The Tim LaHaye Prophecy Study Bible (Associate Editor, AMG Publishers)

ABOUT THE PRE-TRIB RESEARCH CENTER

In 1991, Dr. Tim LaHaye became concerned about the growing number of Bible teachers and Christians who were attacking the pretribulational view of the Rapture as well as the literal interpretation of Bible prophecy. In response, he wrote *No Fear of the Storm* (Multnomah Publishers, 1992; now titled *The Rapture*, Harvest House). In the process of writing this book, Tim was impressed by the Christian leaders who, in Great Britain during the 1820s and 1830s, set up conferences for the purpose of discussing Bible prophecy. In 1992, Tim contacted Thomas Ice about the possibility of setting up similar meetings, which led to the first gathering of what is now known as the Pre-Trib Study Group in December 1992.

In 1993, Dr. LaHaye and Dr. Ice founded the Pre-Trib Research Center (PTRC) for the purpose of encouraging the research, teaching, propagation, and defense of the pretribulational Rapture and related Bible prophecy doctrines. It is the PTRC that has sponsored the annual study group meetings since that time, and there are now over 200 members comprised of top prophecy scholars, authors, Bible teachers, and prophecy students.

LaHaye and Ice, along with other members of the PTRC, have since produced an impressive array of literature in support of the pretribulational view of the Rapture as well as the literal interpretation of Bible prophecy. Members of the PTRC are available to speak at prophecy conferences and churches, and the organization has a monthly publication titled *Pre-Trib Perspectives*.

To find out more about the PTRC and its publications, write to:

Pre-Trib Research Center
P.O. Box 14111
Arlington, TX 76094

You can also get information through the Web site:
www.timlahaye.com